Tom Trimmins started woodworking when he was given his first workbench and tools at eight years old. It's been a lifelong passion ever since. After a childhood of making projects at home and hanging around a local cabinet maker's workshop, he studied furniture-making at degree level in Buckinghamshire. After that he worked for several high-end furniture workshops before starting his own business in 2009.

He started teaching after telling a friend that it was something he really wanted to do. Harbouring his own woodworking ambitions, his friend said that if Tom would teach, he would find a group of interested people to learn. Tom has now been teaching woodwork every week for eight years.

In addition to teaching woodworking classes, Tom makes fine furniture at his workshop on a city farm in Islington, London. He works on commissions or teaches during the day and takes classes in the evening.

Tom is a traditionally trained craftsman, with a modern Japanese and midcentury-influenced style. He lives in Essex, UK.

Working with
WOOD

Tom Trimmins

Working with
WOOD

Build your toolkit, learn the skills and
create stylish objects for your home

SEARCH PRESS

First published in Great Britain 2020
Search Press Limited
Wellwood, North Farm Road,
Tunbridge Wells, Kent TN2 3DR

Text copyright © Tom Trimmins 2020

Photographs by Roddy Paine Photographic Studios, shot on location at the author's studio; except for pages 6, 7, 8, 14, 17, ('cupping' image), 32, 36, 37, 39, 41 (bottom), 82, 84, 86 (centre left, centre right, bottom), 127 (bottom), by Mark Davison; and pages 1, 3 (left and right), 5, 46, 47, 58, 59, 68, 69, 80, 83, 85, 87, 86 (top), 92, 93, 108 (in box) 109, 111 by Stacy Grant.

Photographs and design copyright © Search Press Ltd. 2020

ISBN: 978-1-78221-741-1

Suppliers
If you have difficulty in obtaining any of the materials and equipment mentioned in this book, then please visit the Search Press website for details of suppliers: searchpress.com

You are invited to visit the author's website: tomtrimmins.co.uk

Publishers' note
All the step-by-step photographs in this book feature the author, Tom Trimmins, demonstrating woodwork techniques. No models have been used.

Acknowledgments

Thanks to everyone at Search Press who worked on this book, in particular my very calm editor, Edd, who I really enjoyed working with. I'd also like to thank the photographers Stacy, Gav and Mark, who really captured the atmosphere of my workshop and the furniture made there. Thanks to Liz at Freightliners Farm, for her support over the years, which has been invaluable; for giving me my first woodwork teaching job; and for letting me work on my own projects at the farm when I was just starting out – which is a very difficult phase for any maker.

Dedication

Thanks to the many students that have come to the workshop for my classes over the years. Your input of energy and ideas, and your support for what I do, is truly appreciated.

Measurements
Metric measurements are used throughout this book for the purposes of accuracy. I advise that you adhere to the metric measurements wherever possible to ensure the success of your own projects. If you are using imperial measurements, make sure to convert all the measurements before you begin.

CONTENTS

Workbench

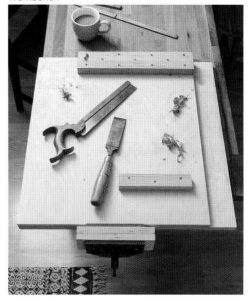

Hook

Box

Decorative shelf

Chest

INTRODUCTION

What could be more satisfying than making your own furniture? Making objects that will add to your feeling of home is an enjoyable thing to do, but where do you start?

Woodworking can seem daunting because there are so many different things you need to know all at once; from which tools and techniques to use to information about the wood itself, and how to design something that will really work. The aim of this book is to guide you in developing your woodworking skills through making beautiful furniture for your home.

All of the projects in this book are made using the hand tools and the handmade work bench described within. Besides the sheer pleasure of using hand tools, there are some practical reasons for avoiding the use of power tools when you are new to the craft. When you are cutting a beautiful piece of wood with the saw, chisel or plane, you learn how the wood responds and become capable of reading the grain. Eventually, you will find yourself seeing, imagining and feeling what will happen with each cut. Using machines from the start would reduce this insight.

I started woodworking as a child, piecing things together out of whatever scrap wood I could get my hands on in my parent's garage, and using random tools borrowed from my dad. The excitement of making something that, not so long ago, existed only in my head never gets old. Woodworking gives me a feeling of connection to people, the forest and to other woodworkers past, present and future – I feel humbled by it.

At first you might find woodworking challenging, but there will be a time when you realise that hours have passed by unnoticed and you are contentedly cutting wood, living in the moment and taking it all in.

Now, let's make some shavings!

Above is a selection of pieces I have made. Wood is wonderfully versatile, practical and beautiful.

WHAT IS WOOD?

'Wood is beautiful and versatile, and
a truly sustainable material.'

Wood is a bundle of fibrous tubes made out of cellulose that are bound together
with a natural glue called lignin. The direction the fibres run within the wood is
called the grain. Wood is strong and easy to work with simple tools, and has
been used for centuries, all over the world, to make tools, buildings, furniture
and works of art.

HARD AND SOFT WOOD

Trees are grouped into hardwoods and softwoods, but this is a botanical
distinction to do with how a tree presents its seeds, rather than the physical
properties of the wood. Hardwoods are generally deciduous, so they lose
their leaves in the winter and have sap rather than resin. Softwoods generally
come from coniferous trees, which have resin rather than sap. Most – but not
all – softwoods are evergreen, with needles rather than broad leaves. They are
a much older type of tree than hardwoods and appeared in the fossil record
before broadleaved trees.
Which type of wood is best to use depends on what you are making.
Generally speaking, those with a medium density – hardwoods like oak, beech,
walnut or ash – are best as they are strong and keep good definition when cut.
Really dense and hard woods will blunt your tools and generally require more
effort. At the other end of the scale, really diffuse softwoods like cedar or spruce
cut very easily bul not necessarily very cleanly.

USEFUL WOOD

Most of the wood used for furniture
comes from the main trunk of the
tree. Immediately beneath the outer
protective bark lies the sapwood –
the living wood. In mature trees, a
layer of older, inert wood usually lies
beneath the sapwood. This is called
the heartwood.

In some species, like oak, the
sapwood is noticeably different from
the heartwood and is susceptible to
insect attack. For this reason, only the
heartwood of such trees is usually used.

Growth rings
*Trees grow outwards, building up in layers around the
centre. Each year of growth creates an early and late growth
ring, visible when you cut through the trunk.*

GREEN AND SEASONED WOOD

When wood is freshly cut it is full of moisture. The cells are moist, squidgy and flexible; and the tree itself full of sap or resin. If it is used in this state, then it is called 'green' or unseasoned wood. After the tree is felled and the trunk is cut into planks, it will lose about half its weight in moislure, taking approximately a year for every 2.5cm to dry.

As the planks dry, the wood can change shape. Wood that was flat when it was green may twist or cup across the width, or bow along the length. This happens because of the way the tree grows: the structure of the growth rings is not consistent through all the planks (see page 14).

Some furniture can be made from freshly-felled green wood; allowances can be made to take account of any timber movements as the wood dries, or some parts can be dried so they fit and don't shrink later. However, when you are making furniture that relies on more precision, such as a chest of drawers, table or door, you need wood at a stable moisture level. If you make something while the wood is still too wet, the wood will continue to shrink after you have finished. Something may crack or twist and joints may break.

The woods you need for making the projects in this book will have been dried: either in a kiln at a consistent temperature, or air-dried outside in a pleasant-sounding process called 'seasoning'. Using dry, seasoned wood means that it is stable and will not shrink or change shape as much once it's dried out – though note that even seasoned wood is not completely stable: it will expand and contract as the weather changes throughout the year.

CHOOSING THE RIGHT WOOD

Woods have different densities and different properties. Some are more suitable for certain uses than others – a cedar table top would be too soft and prone to damage, for example, but using tough, resilient oak or ash would work very well. Practicality is not the only consideration: some pieces of wood are simply beautiful, and careful planning will help to make sure you can make the most of this important quality. When choosing the wood to use for a project, you need to take these differences into account.

These pages look at some traditional uses for different woods, to give you some inspiration and ideas on which you might like to use for your own projects. Whatever you choose, make sure you use good wood for your projects. When you think of the many hours you will invest in a project, it's worth setting out with good-quality materials.

WOOD FOR THIS BOOK

The projects in this book use woods that I have found easy to find locally. If you can't get the species I have used where you are in the world, it is better to use a local equivalent than spend a fortune on getting exactly what I've specified. Whatever you use, be sure that it is high enough quality.

I've used lots of ash in the projects in this book because it's nice to work with: the grain pattern is beautiful and quite easy to follow, which makes it easier to make sure you're cutting in the right direction. Another advantage is that it's inexpensive in comparison with other species.

If you're worried about wasting materials, you could consider using cheap softwood to make a prototype version. This will give you the opportunity to learn from doing it before moving on to using a nicer piece of wood for the final version. If you're short on time, I suggest you just get stuck in. You will likely have to accept that not everything will be perfect about what you've made, but making mistakes is part of the learning process, so don't let this put you off. As you take a moment to understand why you went wrong, you will still find yourself further ahead than you would otherwise have been.

SUSTAINABILITY

The woods I use are of American, European and English origin. Some I harvest myself but the majority I buy in. I avoid using anything grown in the rainforests – anything tropical or exotc – as these trees are best left where they are. Look for endorsement from the Forest Stewardship Council (FSC), or Programme for the Endorsement of Forest Certification (PEFC) when you buy.

— Oak —

There is a reason lots of wooden houses and ships were made of oak. It is super-durable and resists decay as it is full of tannic acid – a natural preservative. It also makes fantastic barrels as oak wood is dense and impermeable.

— Ash —

Ash is one of the most elastic of woods, so it was formerly used for making carts and things that would be knocked around in use. If you sift carefully through any pile of ash boards you'll probably find quite a variation in colours. Some boards will be very dark and interesting, while others are bright and perfectly clean, almost white. In use, ash works very similarly to oak, but it's ever so slightly softer. Ash is just as durable as oak unless it's used outside.

— Cedar —

Cedar is used to keep insects away because of its natural aroma. It is also very light in weight. Cedar is a very stable wood and very easy to to cut. I often use it for the bases of boxes or trays because it'll stay flat and also look amazing – not to mention the beautiful smell!

— Elm —

Elm is used for making things that you don't want to split, like the seat of a Windsor-style chair which has all the legs and backrest bored into it. More unusually, elm wood was used for water pipes until the nineteenth century.

— Beech —

Commonly used for tools and frames for upholstered furniture, beech is also used for kitchenware as it has a natural antibacterial property. Although slightly dull-looking, beech is a really good choice of wood as it is fantastic to work with. Its uniform texture all the way through means that it cuts exceptionally well. It is a pleasure to use. The quarter-sawn face shows lovely grain patterns.

— Douglas fir —

Where I use Douglas fir, it's because I want the piece to stay flat and stable, characteristics this wood is renowned for. The striking contrasting colours of the grain also make it an interesting choice. This wood is commonly used in shipbuilding as it is very stable and strong yet lightweight in long lengths. This wood has a very sweet resinous smell, and stays very straight when seasoned.

— Yellow pine —

Yellow pine is used in all sorts of interior and exterior construction and for furniture, but perhaps most notably for wooden rollercoasters! It is much darker than other pine varieties and cuts very cleanly.

— Tulip wood —

Tulip wood is used for carving rocking horses as it can be built up in large sections and isn't fantastically heavy. As rocking horses are almost always painted, the wood's odd green colour doesn't matter! This wood is very pleasant to work with as it cuts crisply. Usually cheap to buy, it makes a great option for prototyping and testing out ideas.

— Spruce —

Spruce of various species is used for the construction of musical instruments and lots of different interior construction work including furniture. Spruce is not very durable but it is light in weight and moderately strong.

—Walnut—

Traditionally used for fine furniture and even gun stocks, walnut is beautiful and extremely nice to work with. Its rich colour and lustrous grain are qualities that make it an ideal wood for fine furniture making. It also steam bends very reliably, and works well for super-fine joints. These qualities all add up to make it my favourite wood to use in my work.

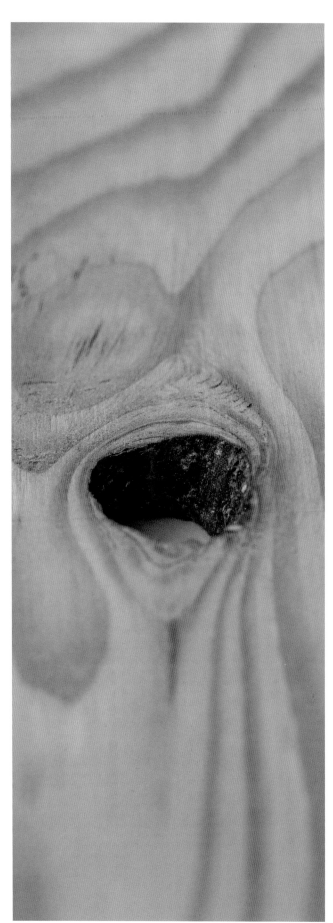

WOOD GRAIN

Learning to read the grain is an important skill in woodworking. The grain will usually run along the length of a board and the wood is strongest in that direction. Think of it like stroking a dog: running your hand the way the fur naturally lies will smooth the fur down, but stroking the wrong way will meet resistance and your hand will lift up all the fibres. Wood grain works a bit like this; and it's worth bearing in mind when we get stuck in with our tools.

Where the grain isn't straight – because of a knot (see below) or side branch, for example, there will often be beautiful colours and patterns, which we can incorporate into our work. Where the grain is uneven, you will have to pay close attention when you're planing the surface smooth or chiselling: if you cut it the wrong way, your blade will tear the fibres.

KNOTS

Knots appear where new wood has been lain down over or around a side branch of the tree, perhaps after the branch has broken off, or just as the tree has grown.

They are accompanied by an area of disturbed grain, usually denser than the surrounding wood – particularly in softwoods. Imagine the fibres of the wood flowing around the knot like a river flowing round a rock.

They make the wood trickier to use, but can be incorporated to add a beautiful effect to a finished object. Note that dead knots – those formed when the tree grows over a broken branch – can fall out, as shown to the left.

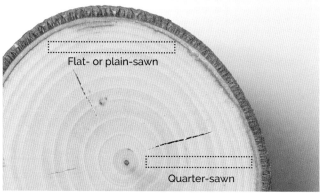

Flat- or plain-sawn

Quarter-sawn

SELECTING BOARDS FOR GRAIN

The most stable boards have quarter-sawn grain, where the growth rings are all at right angles to the face. However, boards that have been plain-sawn are much more common. On these the growth rings have a clear arc when viewed end-on.

WHERE TO GET WOOD

I've always been excited by getting my hands on some new timber – my wife says I have a special 'happy walk' when I've been out buying wood. You might be able to get some wood by reclaiming or recycling some, or you might need to go to the timber yard and buy some. An easy option for small pieces is to buy online via an auction site like eBay.

Buying online can be handy for small pieces, but it is nice to choose wood first-hand to get your imagination going. The easiest way to get properly dried wood is to buy it from a reputable timber yard. Try going to a timber yard near you and see what they are like to deal with. Some are more receptive to hobbyists and smaller orders than others

If you are making smaller projects, you can usually get away with choosing boards that have defects to save some money. If you only need short pieces, for example, a board that's very bowed and would be useless for anything longer could be just perfect for you; it's worth seeing if you can strike a deal.

Hardwoods and fine softwoods are usually bought as boards, sawn when green. As they dry, the wood changes shape owing to the uneven structure of the growth rings and general shrinkage. As a result, the boards are neither straight nor level, and need to be planed true before use.

You can plane your wood by hand but it'll take you a while if you have lots to prepare. Also, if your planing isn't very accurate, it will affect any project you then make with that wood. In my workshop I have machines to prepare the wood which include a planer, thicknesser, table saw and a bandsaw. However, for an easy life I suggest getting the wood machined for you by the timber merchant when you purchase it. If you ask nicely, they will likely still let you choose the boards.

Bear in mind that if you order machined wood, it will likely cost as much to machine the wood as the wood itself costs. Sometimes you will find that a timber yard has a section of machined wood that you can choose from which is pretty much ideal if you're working at home.

Timber yards and builder's merchants

You are looking for a hardwood/softwood timber merchant, which is different from a builder's timber yard (or DIY shop). The latter won't have what you need – although builder's merchants usually stock a selection of machined softwood, which can be useful for some projects.

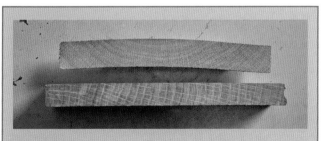

Selecting the right boards

Look at the ends of these two oak boards. The top one was flat-sawn, and shows the pronounced curvature of the growth rings – it has dried and moved in the opposite direction to them. The lower plank, which was quarter-sawn, has growth rings at 90° to the face. This means that it has only shrunk in width as it dried, and so has stayed flat.

Painted ends

Sawn wood is commonly painted at the ends. This stops the board drying too quickly and splitting. This happens because the end of the board, exposed to the air, dries and shrinks at a faster rate than the rest of the board – the wood splits because of this difference.

LOOKING FOR DEFECTS

When choosing wood, look out for the following characteristics, which can cause problems – either in the short or long term. The page opposite shows an example of each defect.

Knot Knots (see page 14) can cause instability and potential weakness. While some can be decorative, you definitely want to avoid large knots in any joints. Smaller knots up to 5–6mm can be less of a less of a problem, depending on where they are located in the piece of wood you using. Always avoid knots when steam bending (see page 65).

Twist Trees naturally twist as they grow, which distorts the wood across its width, height and length. Twist is the least fun thing to remove from a piece of wood, so it is best to avoid buying lengths with a noticeable twist. It is most obvious in longer lengths and more common in certain species, like cherry.

Bow This is curvature along the length of the wood. A little bit is normal, and easy to accommodate in your work. If you come across a really bowed board you can still use it for short pieces, as the bow will be much less noticeable.

Cupping Cupping is where the wood curves across its width. It is a common defect, usually caused by the arrangement of the growth rings in the board. If, when looking at the end of the board, the growth rings look like a happy smile, then the board will cup in the opposite direction – a funny way to remember things, perhaps, but nevertheless true!

End split Wood bought as rough-sawn planks will often have the ends painted or waxed (see page 15) to help avoid end splits. As moisture leaves the end of the board, the end shrinks faster than the rest of the board, splitting it. Some end splitting is normal, and it is a good idea to allow for at least 25mm waste off each end of boards to account for this. After cutting a section off the end of the board, try bending the off-cut. If it easily breaks into pieces, then it's got cracks in it and you need to slice off a bit more.

Rot Rotting wood has started to decay and become compromised. You'll notice it feels quite soft and can be broken easily, even without tools. Rot often makes the wood noticeably lighter, except if it has been in damp conditions, where the wood will soak up moisture instead.

Insect damage Something you might see as you sift through a stack of wood at a timber yard are small holes caused by woodworm, or larger holes caused by big beetles like ash borers. Generally, if the wood has been kiln-dried, then anything living in it will have been killed by dessication, so there's no need to worry if there are a couple of worm or beetle holes. Finding one or two wormholes in the sapwood is common.

Living insects are more of a problem. If the wood has been air-dried or is reclaimed, look for little piles of dust on the surfaces between the boards. These are a sign of active woodworm, so avoid using the affected pieces.

Stick marks These are simply areas of discoloration from how the wood has been dried. The wood is stacked up with little sticks in between called stickers, but sometimes the stickers react with the wood and leave a 'shadow' that has to be cut through before it goes away. If you are unlucky, the mark can be very deep. Stick marks can be hard to spot before the wood is planed.

OTHER DEFECTS

Dried too fast Slightly obscure and much harder to see is wood that has been dried too quickly in a kiln. This creates all sorts of tension within the wood. The fault is most noticeable when sawing the board along the grain. As it is cut, the tension is released and the wood distorts, often pinching the saw blade. There can be quite extreme movement. There is no real way to check for this before cutting up the wood.

Not dried enough Look out for wood which is too wet, which – unlike being dried too fast – is pretty easy to diagnose before you buy it. The board will feel much heavier than a fully-dried board of the same species. You will often be able to feel the moisture as soon as you start cutting the piece, too. The sawdust from cutting wood like this feels damp and smells more aromatic. If you touch the wood to your lips, you'll feel it is moist – you can sometimes even see the moisture within the boards: a drier, lighter band of wood around the outside and a damper, darker core. You can buy a moisture meter in order to check boards for this, but I have never found the need.

Knot

Twist

Cupping

Bow

End split

Rot

Beetle hole

Woodworm holes

Stick marks

TOOLS

AN OVERVIEW OF TOOLS

Tools, lovely tools! Tools have potential; that's probably why they are so attractive – and why they can also be a massive distraction. Even now after a couple of decades of woodworking, I can't resist buying tools.

Note that having expensive tools won't automatically make you a better woodworker, but cheap junk tools will hold you back. My advice is therefore to imagine the cost spread over a lifetime of use, and buy the best you can afford. You will never regret buying good quality and well-designed tools.

With that said, as the average woodworker starting out, buying everything you need in one go can add up to an awful lot of money. Spend a portion of your budget to get the absolute essentials – we look at these over the next few pages – and save the rest until you work out what specifics you actually want from other tools. Buying a plane that's too big, or realizing that you should have bought a slightly deeper saw, is frustrating. If you can resist the temptation, go easy, and avoid getting carried away buying tools on the spur of the moment. Just buy them as you need them and build your collection gradually.

If you've got the cash to buy the absolute best tools, then go right ahead, I wouldn't advise you against it – just know that they won't magically improve your work. A middling-quality tool, set up well, will do most of what you need it to do. This is one of those instances where the time spent working with the tools, understanding them and gaining insight, is more valuable than spending thousands of pounds on top-of-the-range trinkets.

WHERE TO GET THEM

I like to have a mix of old and new tools: older tools, generally speaking, are higher quality and less money. It's pretty easy to get hold of new tools very quickly these days, though physical shops that sell fine tools are rare. Most high-street tool shops and DIY shops simply won't stock what you need, although it's good to know what your local shop has, as it could be handy if you get stuck.

I buy most of my new tools online. If you would like to get hold of some old tools, then the best place to find them is where they are out of context. Shops full of vintage tools tend to know the value of their stock better, while non-specialist antique shops often hide hidden bargains. I like to – rather dramatically! – call tools I find in such places 'lost souls', and it's a great feeling to bring such characterful items back to a workbench and get them cutting wood once more.

CARE AND MAINTENANCE

Having sharp tools is essential for producing good work. Sharpening, or fettling, is just part of the process of woodworking. Although it might at first seem like something standing in the way of actually chopping some wood, it's what enables it to happen well. Instructions for sharpening chisels and plane blades are on pages 36–37, and notes on maintaining saws are on page 24.

- Treat the cutting edges of your tools with great care. They should never bump into each other.

- Rest your chisel bevel side down on the bench so that the edge isn't touching anything.

- Your planes should be nestled on freshly-cut shavings, never on the bench itself, in case there is grit (from abrasive paper, for example) on the surface.

- Clean and polish your tools with WD-40 and machine wax or similar.

A selection of my tools

When I first started out, I wanted my tools to already have a patina of use on them, so, I looked like I really knew what I was doing. Now I like seeing the slow transition from shiny new metal to patinated veteran. It brings to mind thoughts of old jobs done together and conversations with my students.

SAWS

I use a selection of Japanese saws and vintage Western saws. The main difference between them is that Japanese saws cut on the pull stroke and Western saws cut when you push. Aside from the lineage of the saw, you'll see that they have a different number of teeth, as well as different ways to sharpen the teeth.

Japanese saws are great when you're just starting out because straight out of the box they work really well, cut exceptionally cleanly and are very good value. The blades last quite a while as well. You have to be very careful with the finer blades, but you should be treating all of them carefully anyway. If you do happen to damage one by accident, which can happen when you're learning, then you can replace the blade and start again. Although I dislike the disposable nature of this, it is nonetheless practical. The old blades can sometimes be repurposed to make small knives and scrapers. I usually keep them for cutting reclaimed wood where grit or hidden nails might be lurking.

TYPES OF SAW

There are two main types of saws in woodworking: rip saws and crosscut saws. Rip cutting is cutting along the grain, while crosscutting is slicing across the fibres instead of following along them.

Rip If a saw has relatively few teeth, it usually means it is more suited to rip-cutting. This is easy work for a saw as it is moving along the fibres without having to slice across them; it is simply pulling them out of the way. Fewer teeth are better in this instance because you're really just trying to get rid of the material, so the saw has bigger spaces between the teeth, called gullets, in which the waste wood collects. You'll also find that on a rip saw the teeth aren't sharpened to a triangular tip on the end; instead they have a flatter chisel-like edge.

Crosscut You can tell a crosscut saw by the higher number of teeth per inch. Japanese saws are superb at crosscutting: a 22tpi *dozuki*, for example, will leave a surface that is perfectly smooth. Each tooth is sharpened to a fine knife-like tip that cleanly severs the wood fibres. In Western saws, the more fleam angle (see page 23) added, the better it will crosscut.

Some saws will do both rip cuts and crosscuts quite well, but you have to consider that the saw you use depends on the scale of the wood. I often use a very fine crosscut saw for rip cuts when cutting very small joints, for example. At a larger scale, the saw would cut very slowly and become inaccurate.

This detail shows a comparison of teeth from a rip saw (top) and a crosscut saw (bottom).

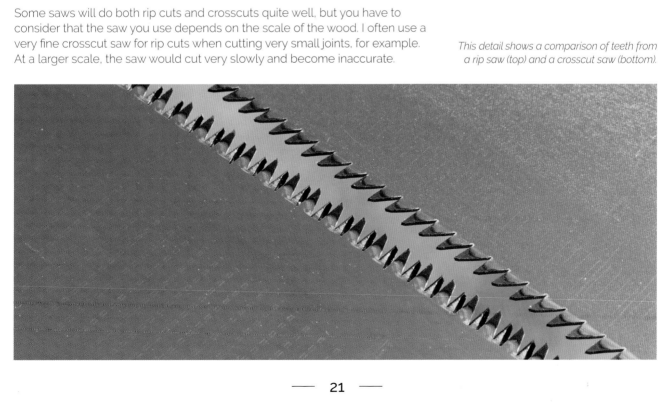

A selection of the Japanese saws I use most frequently. From left to right: rip kataba, *ultra fine* dozuki *22tpi crosscut,* kataba *15tpi crosscut, small* dozuki *18tpi saw.*

A selection of Western saws – these three will form a versatile core for your saw collection. From left to right: dovetail saw, tenon saw, rip cut panel saw.

JAPANESE SAWS

Dozuki A saw with a steel spine like a Western tenon saw. A *dozuki* can have rip or crosscut teeth.

Kataba This type of saw has no back, instead having a thicker blade to add strength. As with the *dozuki*, a *kataba* can have either rip or crosscut teeth.

Kugihiki A flush-cutting saw that is flexed onto the work and has no set (see jargon and terminology, opposite); as a result of which it will not mark the surface.

Ryoba A double-sided saw, with rip teeth on one side, crosscut on the other.

WESTERN SAWS

Panel saw Roughly equivalent to a *kataba* (see left).

Tenon saw Usually quite deep and can be very large, always with a heavy brass or steel back supporting the blade. Sharpened with rip teeth.

Carcass saw Similar in size to a tenon saw – though often not quite as deep – and sharpened with crosscutting teeth.

Dovetail saw A saw with a shallow blade and moderate tpi, sharpened with rip teeth. The low height makes the saw more accurate while the rip teeth let the saw move quickly through the wood, helping to make the sides of the joint smooth.

Coping saw A saw with a thin replaceable blade held in a tensioned frame. Used for cutting curves.

Fret saw/piercing saw A finer version of a coping saw, a piercing saw has a smaller frame. They are ideal for cutting out waste when dovetailing as the blades are very fine.

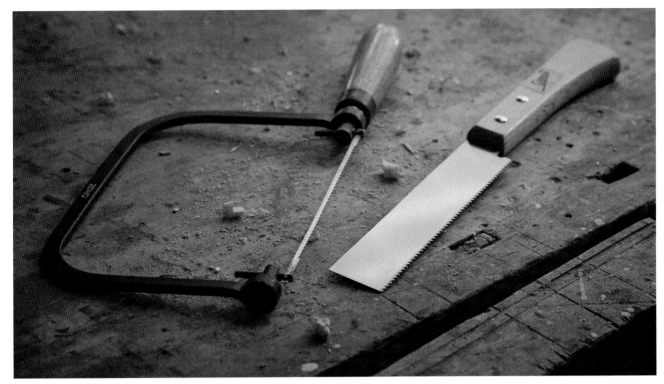

Coping saw (left) and flush-cutting saw (right).

WHAT SAWS DO I NEED?

You don't need to buy a whole pile of saws to start out; just buy a limited selection. You'll need a small *dozuki* 18tpi; a large crosscut *kataba* 15tpi; a rip cut *kataba* 9tpi; and a rip-cutting large *kugihiki* flushcut saw.

Buy quality. You'll find that most cheap tenon saws cut quite a wide kerf as well as having quite large, chunky handles which are pretty uncomfortable to use. I don't like plastic handles at all; they never feel right to me.

Tip

There should be no friction as you cut. A saw that is dragged through a wonky kerf will lose the set on one side and then won't be able to cut a straight line – avoid!

Jargon and terminology

TPI Short for 'teeth per inch', this gives an idea of how coarse or fine the saw is. Generally a rip saw will have fewer teeth than a crosscut saw. My finest crosscut saw is 22tpi while a coarse rip saw is 5 to 7tpi.

Kerf The cut that the saw makes. The kerf is as wide as the saw plate plus the set of the teeth on each side.

Set The teeth of a saw are bent, or set, away from the blade by a fraction of a millimetre, alternately left and right. This allows the saw to pass through the wood without getting stuck. Too much set makes the kerf wide and will cut more slowly as more wood is being removed. It also allows the saw to slop around, making it less accurate. The ideal is a narrow kerf, just wide enough so that it doesn't get stuck. This ensures the saw cuts only what it needs to.

Gullets The space between the teeth is where the wood that has been cut collects as it is propelled out of the kerf by the movement of the saw. A rip saw has fewer teeth so that it can have bigger gullets and remove more waste. On Japanese saws the gullets are very deep which allows lots of waste to clear.

Some other terms you might see

Fleam The angle of the leading surface of the saw's teeth are filed to help them crosscut more cleanly. It is more time consuming to sharpen a saw like this but can give good results. Adding fleam makes the teeth more knife-like.

Rake The angle of the front surface of the saw teeth measured from vertical. Rake has an effect on how the saw handles: a saw with negative rake will be very aggresive, for example.

Progessive rip Some saws have teeth that get bigger the further away for the handle they get. This makes the saw faster but still easy to start and control.

HOLDING YOUR SAW

It is easy to focus solely on your hand holding the saw, but it is important to think about how the rest of your body is positioned too. Your hand, elbow and shoulder should all be in line as you saw, and your feet set shoulder-width apart, one slightly forwards and one back for stability.

Resist the urge to grip the handle too hard. At first you will find that your grip will be too tight – it's a common side effect of concentrating really hard on what you are doing, but overgripping will make the saw track consistently off line. It will also needlessly tire you out. Grip lightly but positively, and every so often relax your hand. The saw should move backwards and forwards in a nice, linear, rhythmical way.

The correct way to hold a Western saw. The wrist and elbow are in line, the grip is relaxed, and the index finger is pointing along the saw – all helping to align your wrist correctly.

SHARPENING SAWS

Japanese saws usually (but not always) come with replaceable blades, so it's simply a case of swapping a blunt one out for a sharp one. The Japanese saws I use in this book all use replaceable blades with a telltale blue tinge from induction hardening and are not resharpenable. Some higher grade Japanese saws can be resharpened, though this is very fine work and you'll be lucky to find a traditional *metate* (a specialist saw-sharpener) to do it for you or teach you.

All Western saws of sufficiently high quality – whether old or new – can be resharpened, so you'll get a lifetime of use out of their blade. You need to use a special vice and triangular files. However, it's a subject in itself, which takes it beyond the scope of this book. Sharpening saws is very skilled work but interesting, so I do encourage you to seek out more information. It will help you learn how saws really work.

The long handle of a Japanese saw allows you to adjust your grip for different purposes. Holding it closer to the blade (left) gives you greater control; while holding it further along the handle (right) increases your leverage and gives you more power.

Holding the saw at the beginning of the cut. Note the positions of the index finger and thumb. The subtle oval shape of the handle helps to align the saw in your hand.

PLANES

A plane is used for smoothing wood and for making it square and flat. The blade of a plane protrudes from a hole in the sole called the mouth. When the sole is run over a surface, the blade shaves away a fine layer of anything standing proud of the surface, equivalent to how much the blade is extended.

The longer the plane, the flatter the surface it can produce. If you imagine the surface of the wood is like a landscape with hills and valleys, a really long plane will rest on the hilltops and bridge over the valleys. It can then gradually cut down through the high spots till they are level with the lowest spots. If you use a short plane, it will just follow the surface and won't smooth out the peaks and troughs at all. Sometimes that's okay; such as when the wood needs only to be smoothed, having previously been made flat with a larger plane.

They come in different sizes, from a tiny no. 1 up to a gigantic no. 8. The sizes are a bit like shoe sizes, even including half sizes. A larger size gives the plane more weight, so you have a bit more momentum in use. However, bear in mind that there is also extra weight to move around.

Planes can be made from iron, bronze or wood, with a metal-bodied plane being easiest to get to grips with when you're starting out. However, I'm a big fan of wooden planes, both old and new. They are refreshingly lightweight and glide well over a surface. It is also worth noting that old wooden planes are often pitifully cheap and yet the blades are often of superb quality. The traditional wedge that holds the blade in place is very effective, and while tapping the plane to adjust it can take some getting used to, it works really well.

WHAT PLANES DO I NEED?

It's helpful to have more than one size of plane, but if I could only have one, then for general use, a no. 5 or a 5½ would be most useful; I would probably go for the bigger rather than smaller size. Having said that, no. 4 planes are really common, so if you already have one, try getting started with that.

Many of the planes I use are second-hand, produced at different times over the last century – some even the century before. For your first plane, try to find a decent vintage no. 5; or treat yourself to a new one.

A selection of common planes

From left to right: no. 4 with Norris-style adjuster; low angle block plane; wooden smoothing plane; no. 5½ iron fore plane; no. 4 transitional plane.

Buying tips

Never buy a vintage plane that has anything missing – the cost of replacing specific parts can equal the cost of the tool. If a plane looks like it has been treated very roughly, it could well have damage that is not immediately apparent.

The cast iron sole of a plane can develop cracks, so inspect it carefully, particularly around the mouth which is the weakest part. If it's so rusty it looks like it's been lurking in the bottom of the sea, then I'd avoid it, as the deep pitting from heavy rust on a blade can prevent it from being sharpened properly. However, light surface rust from lack of use is easily fixed, so if you find one cheap that has only a light coat of rust, go for it! If it turns out to be a dud, then you won't have spent very much.

Be wary of an old tool that is totally unused. Although this can be good, it can also simply mean that it's not a good tool, and so it never got used.

PARTS OF A BENCH PLANE

Sole The flat underside; the surface of the plane that you lay on the wood. Check the sides are square to the sole, otherwise you will have trouble when using the plane on its side on a shooting board (see page 45). The sole should be flat; you can test this with a straight edge.

Mouth The mouth is a hole in the sole, through which the blade emerges. The size of the plane's mouth controls the quality of the cut. If it is very large, it will allow large shavings to pass through – good if you are roughing to size, but if you want really fine shavings, then the mouth needs to be smaller, particularly for wood with uneven grain. The edge of the mouth just in front of the blade is the important bit, as it presses down on the wood just before it is cut. If the mouth is really wide then the wood is not held down as it is cut and will tend to splinter more. Having the mouth adjusted correctly will allow you to plane surfaces that have difficult grain patterns with ease.

Blade The razor-sharp cutting blade of the plane. The back of the blade (the flat side) must be nice and flat and polished so that the chipbreaker will sit snugly against it. Only the last 25mm or so needs to be flattened and polished.

Chipbreaker This sits on top of the blade and makes the shaving break away from the surface as it is cut, allowing you to plane even across uneven grain. It is secured by the chipbreaker screw.

Lever cap This keeps the blade and chipbreaker in position. The contact surface on the underside, where it presses down on the blade, should be checked to ensure it sits nicely on the top of the blade and chipbreaker. The lever cap should never be used as a screwdriver to undo the blade/chipbreaker screw as you can damage it.

Lateral adjuster This slews left or right, allowing you to adjust the blade so that it produces an even thickness of shaving.

Depth adjuster A wheel that you turn to adjust how much the blade protrudes through the mouth, and thus how much wood is being removed with each pass.

Frog This is an angled surface or block that the blade sits on. On a metal plane it is adjustable so that it can be moved backwards or forwards to change the size of the mouth. On a wooden plane, the frog is instead an integral surface so is not as readily adjustable – though it can be altered with paper stuck beneath the blade.

Frog hold-down screws As the name suggests, this holds the frog in place. This should be lightly tightened or you won't be able to adjust the frog.

Frog adjustment screws Not directly visible in the image opposite, these sit next to the depth adjuster. They allow you to reposition the frog while the blade is in position, and see what effect your adjustment is making. The outer two lock the position, while the middle one makes the adjustment. Different planes have different types.

MAKING ADJUSTMENTS

These general notes explain the theory of adjusting your plane; the following pages show the practice step-by-step.

Depth of cut It is easiest to set the depth by looking at what the plane cuts than by looking at the blade itself. If you are taking very fine shavings, you simply won't be able to see how much the blade protrudes. Start with the plane set so that it removes nothing, then incrementally wind the depth adjuster clockwise until it starts to cut. You may then need to make an adjustment for level using the lateral adjuster. Note that the depth adjuster has slack or 'backlash' that you need to keep an eye on. If you wind the blade back in (taking off less wood), then you need to wind it back the opposite way as if you were about to extend it. Otherwise there will be no tension on the mechanism and the blade will gradually shimmy away from the wood as it cuts.

Angle of cut With the plane held upside-down and a light source behind, make your first adjustment by pushing the lateral adjuster towards the side that is sticking out too much. You can then test it by taking a shaving – still upside-down – from a thin offcut. A light tap on the side of the blade with a pin hammer is the best way to make tiny adjustments.

Size of mouth On an iron plane the mouth can be adjusted down in size quite easily by moving the frog forwards.

Flattening the sole If your plane's sole is uneven, it can be flattened with 120 grit paper on a piece of glass, as the iron is relatively soft. Its best to do this with the blade in place but retracted, as when the blade is under tension it changes the shape of the sole. The blade can be protected from metal dust with a bit of masking tape.

Parts of a typical plane

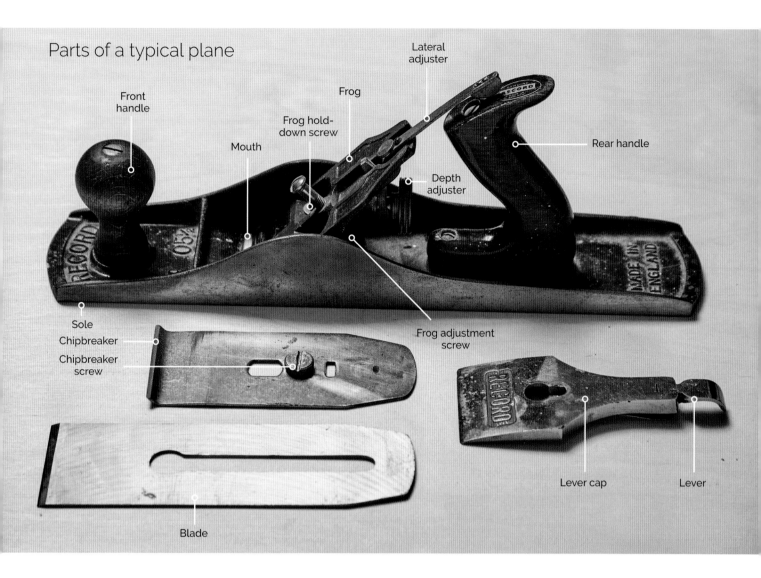

Lateral adjuster

Frog

Front handle

Frog hold-down screw

Mouth

Rear handle

Depth adjuster

Sole

Frog adjustment screw

Chipbreaker

Chipbreaker screw

Lever cap

Lever

Blade

Wooden planes

On a wooden plane, the blade is held in with a wedge. Adjusting the depth involves tapping it with a mallet or a small pin hammer. If you want to increase the cutter depth, you can simply tap the top end of the blade to poke it out a bit more – just do it incrementally so that you don't go too far. To take off less, hold the plane with the front end upright in the air and, whilst supporting the blade and wedge with your hand (in case it falls out), tap the striking button. This is usually on the back end of the plane. Once you make an adjustment like this, you will need to give the wedge a tap to reseat everything.

If the mouth of a wooden plane is too big, you will need to cut extra pieces of wood to close it up. When you're first starting out, it's not the sort of thing you want to be taking on.

Note that the sole of a wooden plane should be planed or scraped flat – if you use sandpaper, the grit can lodge in the sole and then migrate to the wood you are working on, which will blunten your blade.

Jargon and terminology

Double iron A plane with a chipbreaker.

Single iron A plane without a chipbreaker; usually applied to specialist types like scraper, rebate and moulding planes.

SETTING UP YOUR PLANE

The steps below will walk you through how to set up a typical bench plane correctly. Before you begin, make sure the blade is razor-sharp (see pages 36–37). Above all else this makes the most difference. If you can't take super-fine shavings, then it's almost certainly because your plane is not sharp, though there can be other things in play, such as the sole not being flat, the chipbreaker set incorrectly, or the frog or other screws not being tightened enough.

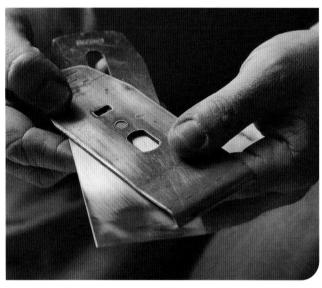

1 Place the chipbreaker on the blade. Be careful not to drag the chipbreaker over the cutting edge as you slide it into place.

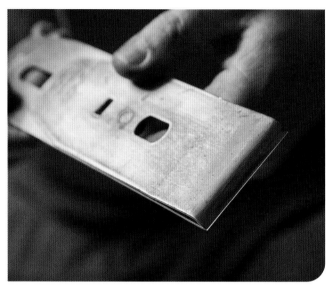

2 Tighten the screw up a little so that there is some tension but you can still move things around, then adjust the chipbreaker until it is 0.5mm back from the cutting edge. If it is too far away from the edge, it just won't do anything.

3 Slot the blade and chipbreaker 'double iron' through the mouth very carefully and make sure that it is seated on the adjuster prongs and sitting flat on the frog. Drop the lever cap on top.

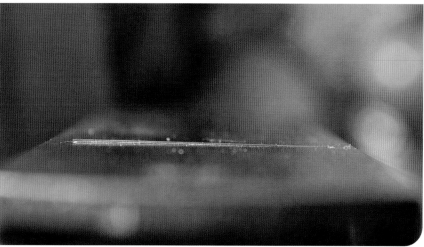

4 Tighten the lever cap in place, then hold the plane by the front handle and turn it over. Get a light source behind you so that you can see the leading edge of the blade (as shown to the right). If you can't see the blade, try turning the adjuster to extend it more. Do an initial levelling of the blade with the lateral adjuster (see page 28); the blade can then be fine-tuned by trying it out. Note that the plane is set to take a fine shaving – ideally the blade should protrude only a tiny way. It's best to start from cutting nothing, and very gradually wind the adjuster to extend the blade until it cuts.

The assembled plane

Be sure not to put the sole down flat on the bench as any grit on the surface will damage the cutting edge. Equally, it is best not to put the plane down on its side, as once you have put it down like this a dozen times, it can knock the blade out of level. Once I've got a few wood shavings going, I make a little nest for the plane to sit on that protects it.

HOLDING YOUR PLANE

The plane is normally held with your dominant hand on the back handle and the other one on the front handle, as shown above.

Sometimes, however, I grip the edge of the casing next to the front handle instead for more control, as shown to the right. This is the grip used for adjusting edges to be square. Applying gently pressure to the left or right allows you to control where the wood is removed: watch which part the shaving takes off. Dragging your finger along the edge of the board, as shown, will help you to keep the plane level.

OTHER TYPES OF PLANE

All you need is a bench plane and a block plane to make the projects in this book, but there are some interesting specialist planes that are ideal for when you move on or decide to experiment.

Combination plane Used for making grooves and simple mouldings, combination planes come with a set of blades for different profiles and even a matched tongue and groove cutter. I have a no. 50 and a no. 45, which I find useful for cutting grooves in small pieces; though I rarely use the moulding cutters.

Apron plane Tiny but very handy, an apron plane is simply a plane small enough to fit in an apron pocket. Keep one with you to whip out if you need to reveal the grain of a board in the timber yard or do a tiny chamfer.

Rebate plane A rebate, or rabbet, is a step in the edge of a board. This plane has adjustable fences to set the width and depth that is cut, allowing you to make such rebates. I also sometimes use this plane without the fences for making panelled doors or smoothing very large tenon cheeks.

Scraper plane Used for smoothing the surface, with similar results to a handheld cabinet scraper (see page 40), but without the burning thumbs! A scraper plane is really useful for situations where the grain direction of a board makes it awkward to smooth. The simple type pictured, the Record or Stanley no. 80, is pretty easy to set up.

Shoulder plane Used for cleaning the shoulders of tenons and sometimes the cheeks too.

Router plane A precursor to the modern electric router, a router plane has a blade that can be set to the required depth and then used to remove waste in the bottom of a housing or dado. It can also be used for inlay work and for trimming tenon cheeks.

Specialist planes

A selection of some of the more unusual planes I own. Some see more action than others, but all are useful.

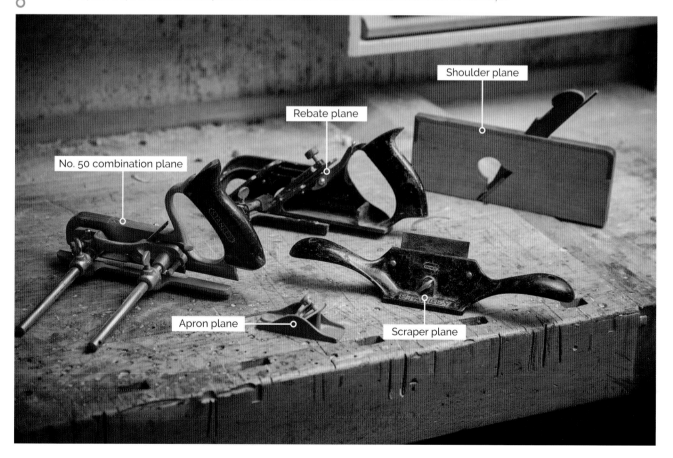

Shoulder plane

Rebate plane

No. 50 combination plane

Apron plane

Scraper plane

CHISELS

A chisel is such a simple tool, but you can really do a lot with it. Used for all manner of trimming, paring, chopping, carving and shearing cuts, the only complex parts of this tool are the hands that direct it.

Tools made for skilled craftspeople tend to be finer, whilst many low- to mid-quality modern tools are simply made to survive misuse. I'd recommend trying lots of different types to find out what you like. In general, I prefer old chisels with wooden handles, as old steel is mostly very good quality and the tools tend to be more finely made. However, while plastic handles never sit so well in the hand, they are tough if you've got lots of chopping to do – with a mallet striking the handle, durability is key.

WHAT CHISELS DO I NEED?

Chisels come in different widths. A single 25mm wide chisel is very versatile, but you will do best with a range of sizes, as shown on this page.

As with planes, buying old chisels can be a cheap way of getting a really high-quality tool. Generally, any chisel you buy second-hand in the UK will probably be made in Sheffield, and of decent quality. I'm not really worried about the condition of the cutting edge, as that is easy to repair (see pages 36–37). However, I will check that the chisel has not been bent by being used as a lever or been worn away unevenly by being sharpened on a stone that isn't flat. I also avoid anything that's really rusted with deep rust pits on the underside of the blade. If it's pitted you'll have to cut through all the pitting and so that it doesn't leave a blunt patch on the edge of the blade.

Avoid a chisel if there is only 25–50mm of blade left. If the handle is broken, they can be replaced, but generally I just try and find ones with unbroken handles for an easy life.

A selection of chisels.

From top to bottom: 6mm chisel, bevel-edged with boxwood handle; 9mm Marples chisel with splitproof handle; nice fine 12mm bevel-edged chisel with a boxwood handle; 20mm Axminster 'Rider' brand chisel with hornbeam handle; 25mm firmer chisel by Marples with workshop-made octagonal oak handle.

HOLDING YOUR CHISEL

The chisel is always used with two hands except when used with a mallet. Hold the chisel in your dominant hand (for me my right hand), and use your other hand to position, stabilize and control it. I usually have a grip on the side of the chisel as shown in the picture, but I alter my grip to suit the circumstances. Don't let your dominant hand creep up the handle, as in most cases this will give you less control.

If you are using the chisel with a mallet for chopping, rest the chisel slightly on one of the corners of the cutting edge. You can then 'walk' it into the right position, rocking from corner to corner as needed. This makes it easier to position.

When you put the chisel down on the bench, place it bevel down so the cutting edge will not be resting on anything and it will be less likely to be damaged by specks of grit.

Sharpening stones (left) and leather loaded with buffing compound (above).

SHARPENING PLANES AND CHISELS

When sharpening, the aim is to produce a bevel that is at the correct angle and a back that is flat. Gradually finer grades of abrasive stone are used until the surfaces of the blade back and bevel are polished to a mirror finish.

At a minimum, you will need two sharpening stones, of different abrasive grades. These can be of different compositions. I recommend starting off with a diamond stone that has 400 grit on one side and 1,000 grit on the other, and a fine polishing stone: anywhere between 3,000 and 6,000 grit will do it. I use a ceramic stone here, but diamond is fine, too.

It is possible to sharpen chisels and plane blades freehand, but after doing this for years and then switching to using a honing guide (see below), I can say that the jig is much more consistent. A basic honing guide can be bought for very little, or you can spend a lot more. The one I recommend and use myself in the workshop is by Veritas: it's well made and has several different attachments, such as the narrow chisel holder which make it even better. The technique I use for sharpening with a jig, explained opposite, is very similar for both plane blades and chisels.

A honing guide is a tool or jig that holds the blade at the correct preset angle and keeps it square in relation to the sharpening stone.

The angle checker is a simple tool for checking the sharpening angles of your tools.

1 Make a 25° primary bevel on the blade using a super coarse stone. This gives you the initial shape of the edge. If you have access to one, a high-speed bench grinder or linisher makes this step much easier and more consistent.

2 Place the blade in the honing guide and use the angle setting attachment to set the angle to 30°.

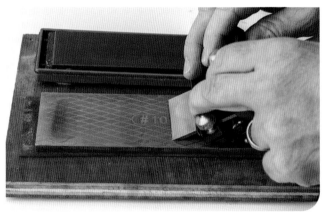

3 Add a little lubricating oil to the sharpening stones. Avoid viscous oils. Here I'm using WD-40, but water will also work as long as you have never used oil on the stone before.

4 Pressing firmly, roll the jig back and forth along the diamond stone to hone the edge on the 1,000 grit side. Repeat on the fine polishing stone to sharpen it further. You will feel a burr on the flat side of the blade when you have sharpened it enough.

5 Remove the jig. The width of the honing bevel will increase as the plane is sharpened multiple times. When it gets really wide, it makes honing slower, so the blade should be reground to remove some of this metal. Place the flat of the blade on the sharpening stone and move it in small circles. This will remove coarse scratches in the surface that make it impossible to get a super-sharp edge. Repeat on the finer stone. You will see the burr break away.

The sharpened blade, ready to use. Note the mirror finish on the cutting edge. The cutting edge can be further enhanced by using a leather strop and buffing compound to consolidate and polish the edge.

CORDLESS DRILL

Using a cordless drill is the easiest way to drill holes and drive screws. A hand-powered drill is slower and requires both hands to operate the drill, instead of having one free to hold the work. These days, excellent cordless drills are available for a small amount of money, and can be used for everyday DIY as well as your woodwork. I recommend that you get yourself a decent cordless drill with at least two batteries. In my workshop I've got Makita and Bosch drills, though I'd happily use other brands – they just happen to be what I've used for years.

The drill speed/torque is selected on the top of the drill. You'll see a button which usually has one or two settings. This is a gearbox, so slower speeds will result in a higher turning force; useful for driving screws (particularly bigger ones). The higher speed setting has a lower turning force; perfect for drilling holes where you're trying to clear the wood out of the hole. As the drill spins faster, it's much more efficient. Always make sure that the drill is stopped when you change gear. In addition to the gearbox, most cordless drills also have a slower screwdriver function which engages a mechanical clutch. This is something I only ever use when drilling big holes. For safety, I prefer to work by feel.

If you're planning to use your drill only intermittently at home, and there will be periods when it's not used, you're better off buying the newer battery types, such as lithium-ion, as they hold their charge even when used infrequently.

When compared with tools like hand planes, which will last for many lifetimes, it's easy to think of drills as almost disposable. In some ways this is true, but if you choose good quality power tools they last quite a while as well as making life so much easier and the work much quicker. The first drill I bought is still going strong ten years later, with only a change of batteries needed. Some people feel that a cordless drill is not a 'proper' hand tool but I think this is simply not true. I certainly appreciate how much easier it has made my work over the years.

Safety
Never risk drilling towards your hand as you may go deeper than you expect. Tuck in any loose clothing and long hair so it can't get wrapped around the drill.

Whatever drill you choose, make sure you have at least one spare battery.

DRILLS AND SCREWS

There is nothing wrong with the careful use of screws in a project but they must be applied very carefully. Generally speaking, any screws I use in a piece of furniture are either hidden underneath or otherwise out of sight. Where they are on show, I use slotted brass screws, though I always buy the same size of screw in steel. This lets me use the much stronger steel screw to cut a thread for the brass screw and then swap them over. Brass screws should only be driven by hand, as this allows you to feel if there is any flex in the screw as you rotate it – that is an indication that it might be about to snap.

When buying screws, I recommend getting a selection of different sizes, instead of walking to the hardware store every time you need a different size. Diameters of 3.5mm and 4mm are the ones I use the most as they are quite narrow and drive in easily.

I also buy steel Pozidriv head screws. These very strong screws allow more torque to be applied, and are fully threaded along their length. Lubricated with wax, they are yellow passivated to make them more resistant to corrosion. As a result, they appear more of a gold colour.

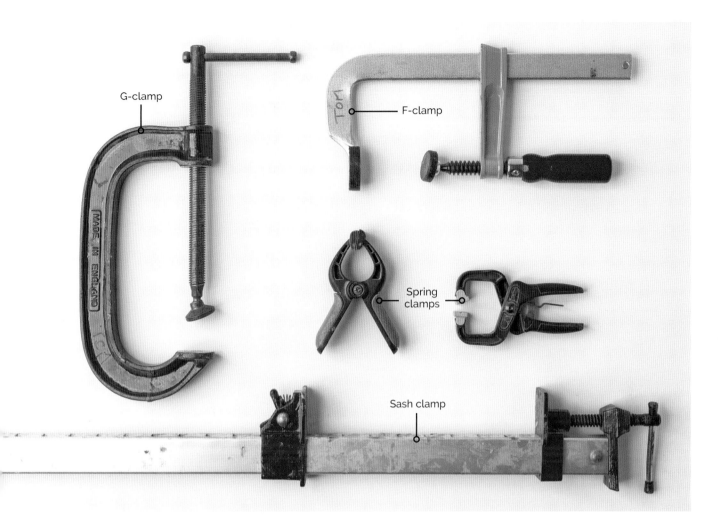

G-clamp

F-clamp

Spring clamps

Sash clamp

CLAMPS

Unlike a vice, a clamp is mobile and has lots of uses besides holding wood, such as applying pressure when gluing, or holding identical components together so the joints can all be marked at the same time. They are easiest to use if they have plastic or cork jaws to stop them marking or reacting with the wood. Scraps of ply can also be taped to the clamp faces and used for this purpose.

Use clamps that are the right size for the job: too big and they will distort everything with their weight; too small and it either won't fit or you will push the clamp beyond what it is designed for.

G-clamp G-clamps can apply a huge amount of force – although this is not always a good thing. If you have to apply vast amounts of pressure to a joint as you are gluing it up, it probably means it doesn't fit properly.

F-clamp So-called because they look like a letter F from the side, the reach of the jaws and the length differ. These are my favourites, and see a lot of use. 220mm capacity is a very useful size to have.

Small clamps A few small spring clamps and ratchet clamps like these are useful for quick, small jobs and repairs.

Sash clamp Sash clamps are long clamps for gluing together panels and frames. I find an aluminium clamp, being lightweight, won't distort your work. Iron clamps can react with and stain the wood if glue seeps out where the bar touches the work.

OTHER TOOLS

These tools can be overlooked because they're not quite as exciting as planes, chisels and saws, but they're just as important. In particular, marking and measuring are the cornerstone of good woodwork. You could cut the highest quality saw kerfs and pare the best edges ever with a chisel, but if all the marking was off when you go to assemble the joint, it will be junk. The tools you need for marking are not necessarily expensive.

Combination square A very useful tool that can mark 45° and 90° angles, with an adjustable ruler that can be used as a crude marking gauge. The built-in level bubble also comes in handy.

Engineer's square Made entirely out of steel, these are superior to traditional wood and metal squares, which.are made with a steel blade and wooden and brass stock (the fat bit). As the materials move around at different rates, such squares tend to go out of true. Being made of just one material, an engineer's square expands and contracts at the same rate.

Sliding bevel gauge This is used for marking and transferring angles.

Awl A stiff metal spike that is used for marking the position of holes.

Steel ruler Choose a ruler that measures in millimetres and starts from the end of the ruler. Avoid a shiny one, as they can be hard to read.

Marking gauge A tool for marking lines parallel to an edge, along the grain. This deceptively simple tool is basically a block of wood with a stick through it and then a pin knocked through the stick.

Cutting gauge Similar to a marking gauge, this tool has a blade instead of a pin. The cutting gauge is used for marking across the grain as it slices across the fibres and thus gives a cleaner finish. It is particularly useful for marking joints on the ends of pieces of wood such as dovetails: a marking gauge can't be used for marking across the grain as the pin tends to tear fibres – even if it looks okay when you've just done it, when you apply finishing oil to your work you will see that the line is broken, giving a messy result. You might also like to try a wheel-type cutting gauge, which does the same job but is easier to handle.

Utility knife A fixed blade knife, such as a Stanley knife, is used for marking.

Tape measure You'll be using this frequently, so invest in a good-quality 5m-length one, preferably only measuring in millimetres, for clarity.

Cabinet scraper A cabinet scraper is a hardened piece of steel that has a sharp burr formed along its edge. This allows you to remove material very easily for smoothing and shaping surfaces. It is like a mid-ground between sanding and using a plane. Unlike a plane, there is a much lower risk of the grain tearing if you go the wrong way. I like a 1mm thick scraper as it is less likely to put hollows in your work by flexing it too hard. You can cut your own from old saw blades, which is a nice idea but can take a while. They are not expensive tools anyway, so I think it is easier to just buy them.

Burnisher The burnisher is a hardened steel or carbide rod, used to sharpen the cabinet scraper (see page 114 for the method).

NOT PICTURED

Oil and wax I use WD-40 to lubricate and protect my tools, and also on sharpening stones when honing them. It slowly evaporates without leaving a residue like oil would and I find the smell pleasant, too. I use machine wax to stop tools rusting and as lubrication on plane soles to help them glide. Normal wax polish will do a similar job.

Glue I have used lots of different glues – currently I favour Titebond 3, which dries a similar colour to many woods. Because of this, if there are any tiny gaps, it hides them more than a clear-drying glue would. I also use five-minute quick-drying PVA which is great when there are lots of things to glue up or when time is short.

Rasps and files Rasps are used for shaping wood. I find the finer half-round ones most useful. I have files for metal and files for wood and don't interchange them. A nice wide, flat second-cut file is great for flattening joint surfaces or for refining a surface after you have used a rasp to shape it. Both rasps and files are available as fine second-cut or bastard which is the coarsest.

Abrasive paper Abrasive papers are commonly available in rolls or packs of a particular grade. The grade number tells you the number of grains in a square inch of paper: the higher the number, the smaller and finer the grit. When sanding you work through the grits, starting with low numbers and working up, gradually refining the surface. I use grey aluminium oxide paper with a no-load coating that stops the dust clogging it up. To start with, 120, 180, and 240 grit will be a good enough selection. To take your sanding to the next level, get some 150, 320 and 500 grit paper in addition. You want enough paper on hand so that you aren't mean about using it: once it loses its bite, it's best to switch to another piece.

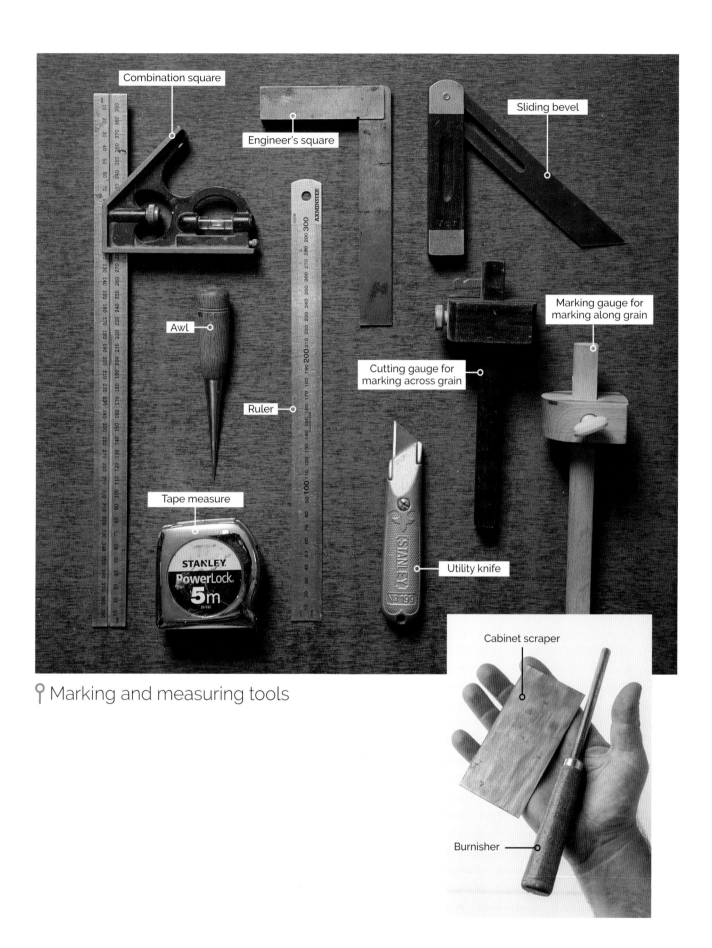

Combination square

Engineer's square

Sliding bevel

Awl

Marking gauge for marking along grain

Cutting gauge for marking across grain

Ruler

Tape measure

Utility knife

⚲ Marking and measuring tools

Cabinet scraper

Burnisher

GETTING STARTED

The workshop is more than just a place where you can make things; it's a place of ideas and concentration. We can create that space whether you're on a kitchen table, outside in your garden, or in a dedicated space like a garage or a shed (lucky you!). It's the ideas and enjoyment that are the important part.

I don't want you to worry about having a workshop equal to the most beautiful one you've seen and dreamt about. Just consider a traditional Japanese workshop: there is no bench; all the work is done simply sitting on the floor or working on trestles or boards. Perhaps this helps you see your space in a new light?

FINDING A SPACE

Starting out, keep your workspace very simple. You can adapt and redesign it as you work out what you really need. If you've got a kitchen table to work on, that will be fine for getting started. If you've got space for a good solid workbench, then that's great. If your workspace is outside (in a garage, for example), avoid contaminating your working area with gritty dust and metal filings as they will embed in the work surfaces and blunt your tools.

The workshop should ideally be dry and of an even temperature. Damp conditions will rust your tools and make any wood you are working on expand, causing cupping and bowing (see pages 16–17). Heat will also have a similar effect, causing wood to shrink, so store wood and wooden tools away from sources of direct heat – whether from the sun or from radiators or heaters.

Ideally, you will find a space where you don't have to put everything away between the times you work, but use what you have.

TOOL CARE

Tools that are well cared-for will stay sharper for longer and give you better results. You should have some kind of box or roll to keep your tools in; and some space to keep them in a dry place. Avoid anywhere really warm as it can loosen tool handles and make wooden tools change shape as it will dry them out.

It sounds mean, but be wary about lending a good tool to someone that might not know how to use it properly.

SAFETY

When you're working, be wary of your surroundings. Don't set yourself up where someone can walk up and surprise you as you're doing some delicate task or where a child or pet will run up to you without you being able to put down your tools.

Try to make your environment calm. Avoid working when you're tired or can't give your full concentration – though if you still want to work on your projects, such times are good for doing things like sanding, where there's not so much opportunity to have an accident.

WORKSHOP APPLIANCES

There are a few simple things that you can buy to help you hold the wood while you work on it. However, some are simple to make, and creating some of these things yourself will help you get to grips with your new tools – that's what the next part of the book is about.

You can make these work-holding devices using pretty basic materials such as plywood and machined softwood that you can get from most DIY shops and places that stock builder's supplies. If you make the bench hook and shooting board on the following pages and buy a vice, you will have all you need to make the other projects in this book.

Bench hook A bench hook (pictured below) is nothing more than a simple board with a couple of cross pieces attached to it for supporting your workpiece as you saw and chisel it. It is used for holding wood while you work on it with chisels or saws. It's a great way of holding small pieces, as the backing block can catch your chisel when you cut through the work. It also has the effect of resisting the force of the saw as you cut. The square end of the cross piece can be used to guide your saw for a square cut.

Shooting board Similar to a bench hook, a shooting board has a few extra parts and is made with extra accuracy. It lets you use a plane to square the ends and sides of boards. Once the shooting board is adjusted properly, it is possible to cut perfectly square edges. The plane is laid on its side and slid along a piece of wood pushed up to the edge of the plane and held square by a cross piece. The shooting board I usually use in the workshop I made over a decade ago.

Vice A stationary work-holding device, a vice is usually attached to something else (like your workbench) to stop it moving while you are working. Although woodworkers haven't always used vices, they do make life much easier. They can be bought fairly cheaply, so I'd recommend getting hold of one and fixing it to a block of wood so that it can be clamped securely to a table or other surface to bring it up to the correct height. There's no need to spend a fortune on a special vice at this stage. There are a few different types available, but at first you will need just a simple bench vice.

A vice will also often have holes that hold removable pegs, called 'dogs', that can be used along with holes drilled in a bench surface to hold bigger components down. I use mainly wooden vices but I also like simple metal ones, usually the larger the better. Make sure that the inside surfaces of the wooden jaw liners stay clean. You can add some thin cork sheet to them for extra grip.

WORKBENCH

A good way to start your foray into woodworking is by making this multipurpose workbench. It will give you something to work on and a way of holding things safely whilst working on them. Making this will teach you vital skills such as measuring and marking accurately, using saws, drilling and planing.

An amalgamation of a shooting board, bench hook, vice and work surface (see page 45), my idea was to give you something you can work on that is both small enough to put away easily and solid enough for serious use. I made everything in this book by using this small workbench. A small vice like the one I've used here is lightweight and easy to move around. Although it lacks the capacity of something bigger, it will still be very useful. Using a larger one will make the workbench more cumbersome to store, and isn't necessary.

I've used a quarter sheet of birch ply for the base because it is dense and well-made yet not too expensive. It cuts very cleanly and screws fix into it well. Another plus point is the thick face veneer which makes it more durable. You could use another type of plywood if you can't get birch ply where you are, but choose something good quality. Some cheap plywoods have thin, perfect veneers on the surface, but are made from very soft cheap wood and are a mess of voids and overlapping layers inside. Have a look along the edge of the sheet and check there are no defects.

The other parts are yellow pine offcuts. You could use many different medium-density woods, such as beech, ash or even plywood for this. Softer woods will tend to wear more quickly and your screws might come loose, but will still work fairly well.

You will need

— Birch ply: 1200 × 600 × 18mm
— 525 × 30mm length of yellow pine
— Saws: small *dozuki* or other crosscut saw, large crosscut *kataba*, coping saw
— Two 200mm F-clamps
— Cordless drill and 4mm dowel point bit, 2–5mm HSS deburring countersink and a PZ2 screwdriver bit and holder
— Screws: 4 × 30mm and 4 × 40mm PZ2 head
— Engineer's square 100mm or bigger
— Pencil and ruler
— Vice, 150mm jaws
— Utility knife

Standard sizes

Birch ply is typically available in 2440 × 1220mm sheets but you can sometimes buy a half or quarter sheet. For this project, it is easiest to start with a neatly cut quarter sheet. Don't assume that the ply is exactly a quarter of a sheet: check the measurement.

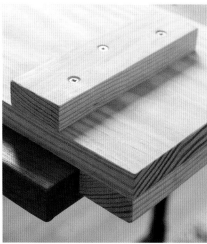

The finished board, ready to use.

Workbench jargon and terminology

Base — The main body, consisting of two pieces of ply screwed together underneath.

Track — The channel the plane runs in (whilst used on its side).

Planing stop — The large cross piece the workpiece rests against as it is cut.

Front stop — The small movable piece at the front of the base that is used for sawing and chiselling.

Table rest — Allows the whole thing to hook onto the front of whatever you are resting it on.

Jaw liners — Plywood pieces fixed to the inside of the vice to stop it marking the work.

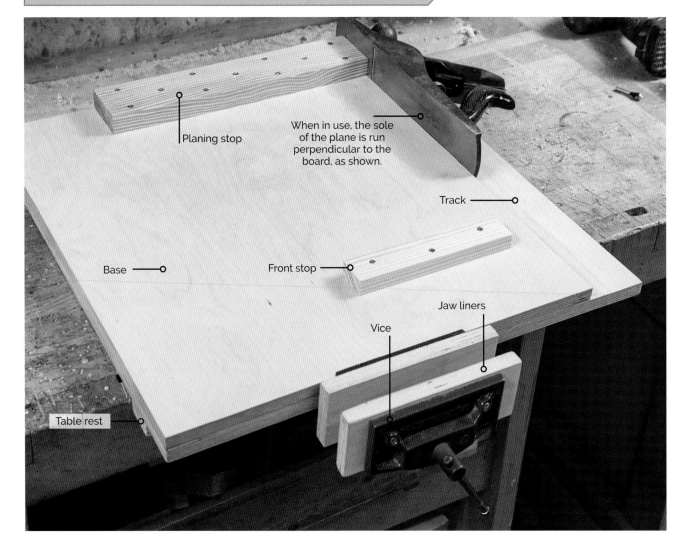

Planing stop

When in use, the sole of the plane is run perpendicular to the board, as shown.

Track

Base

Front stop

Jaw liners

Vice

Table rest

1 Place the plywood on your work surface. Measure the width and make two pencil marks, each 600mm from the end of the board. Line up a long ruler or tape measure to draw a pencil line across the mark, forming a square.

2 Turn the wood so the line overhangs the edge of the work surface, then use clamps to secure it to your surface, as shown. Secure the wood firmly with another clamp on the other side. Leave clear space around the line to be cut.

3 Use the first knuckle of your index finger to guide the large crosscut saw to the correct starting place. You can bend your finger to alter the position. Prepare to saw very lightly in the direction the teeth cut (when using a Japanese saw, it cuts when you pull).

MAKING LONG CUTS WITH A SAW

I'm using a Japanese saw with crosscut teeth to cut plywood, but you could use a ripsaw if you were cutting a strip of wood off a solid board, for example. Here I'm working on a tall bench but you could equally work on something low, which might even be better.

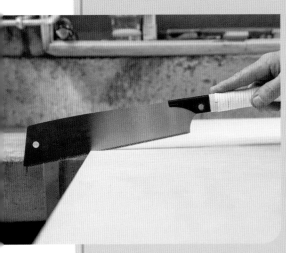

4 Holding the saw near the blade for control, tilt it to 10–15° as shown and gently draw the blade backwards to begin the cut.

5 As you continue cutting, blow any dust away so you can always see your line. If the blade starts to stutter, you're using too much force. Keep the saw at the same low angle as you work.

6 Support the wood as you cut it, especially as you near the end. Use your hip to steady it, get someone else to help you for a minute, or support the piece by turning it round on the worksurface or propping it up. Drop the angle of the saw to near horizontal as you reach the end and saw gently. This helps to reduce the stress on the last fibres being cut.

7 Put the cut-off square, which should measure 600 × 600mm, to one side. Mark a line at 525mm on the remaining wood.

8 Use the large crosscut saw to cut along the line. To help get a straight cut, look down along the saw with your dominant eye. If it is fully upright, you should see only the top of the saw, not the sides.

9 This cut will give you two pieces: a piece measuring 600 × 525mm, which is the top part of the base, and an offcut piece measuring 600 × 95mm, which we will use for the jaws for the vice (see steps 26–30).

Machine-cut edge

Why align like this?

Aligning the machine-cut edges to the side ensures that the channel for the plane will be straight, even if our hand-sawing is a little off.

10 Clear off any sawdust, then place the base on top of the fence as shown. Make sure the edge that will become the edge of the planing track is one of the original machine-cut edges. Draw a line down the overlap so it is easy to put the pieces back together the same way later.

DRILLING AND JOINING WITH SCREWS

Screws are an easy way of joining wood together, especially things that might need to be repaired or adjusted later. They can also be used a bit like an integral clamp on things that would otherwise be awkward or time-consuming to put together.

When fixing one piece of wood to another, a clearance hole equal to the screw diameter is drilled through the first piece. If you are using 4 × 40mm screws, your clearance hole size should be 4mm. This stops the screw threads biting into the first piece and forcing it away from the piece to which it is being attached. The screw threads do not need to engage in the piece you are screwing through; they only need to bite when they hit the wood you are screwing into.

It's a good idea to drill pilot holes in thin wood or when working close to the edge or end. Using large screws is another reason. Measure the core of the screw, which is the diameter minus the threads, to work out what size to use. Pilot holes are not always needed. Some compression of the wood fibres around the screw can be useful as it makes it hold better.

Countersunk screws have a conical head that can be set flush with the surface. To use these you will also need a countersink bit to cut a matching conical hole in the surface.

Get yourself a really nice countersink and it will make everything look much neater. 'Snail' type deburring countersinks, more usually used for metal, are far superior to the traditional 'rose' variety, which tend to leave a hole which is not uniform. Available in different sizes, here I am using a 2–5mm countersink. I like to countersink both sides of a clearance hole – the side where the screw head sits and on the joining surface. This gives a space for any debris or puckering of the surface when the screw is driven in, and prevents the pieces pulling apart from each other.

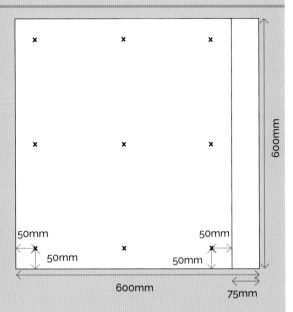

After you have marked all four corner screw positions, simply find the middle points between them to mark the remaining ones. I haven't given you a measurement for this as your project might be a slightly different size from mine.

11 Remove the top piece and mark the screw holes as per the diagram above. Mark each with a cross, so that you have a precise centre point to drill.

12 Put some scrap wood under the main piece, then use the 4mm bit to drill clearance at each of the points marked.

13 Change to the countersink bit and countersink each hole in turn. Next, turn the piece over and countersink the other sides of the holes. This provides somewhere for any debris to collect when you screw the piece together.

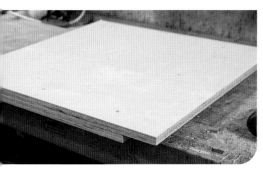

14 Place the 600 × 600mm piece on top of the 600 × 525mm piece (above left), aligning the machined edges as shown in step 10; then clamp the pieces together and secure together with the 4 × 30mm screws (above right). Avoid overdriving screws so they pull down lower than the countersunk cut-out: it looks awful. This is often caused by trying to use the screws to pull a badly fitting piece into shape or by lack of control of the drill speed.

15 Turn the whole thing over. This gets the main piece to a point where you can start working on it – you can finish the rest of the project on top of it.

MEASURING AND MARKING: USING THE ENGINEER'S SQUARE

To make my saw start easily in the right place I like to make a shallow notch on the corner of the wood with my knife, as shown here. The straight cut exposes part of the finished surface so that the saw can run against it; the angled cut makes the saw slide down against the other straight side, again helping you to start sawing in the right place. The other trick when you start sawing is to do so very gently.

I prefer to use all-metal engineer's squares, as they keep their shape where traditional wood and steel squares do not.

Always hold the square in a comfortable position. Move the wood around rather than holding the square in an awkward way. Your thumb should be in the middle of the stock (the fat bit). Don't let it creep up towards the corner as then the square will move as you mark against it. Use your index finger to pin the blade (the thin part of the square) to the surface you are marking to stop it moving as you mark against it.

16 Place the yellow pine on your partly-made bench surface and check that one end of it is square. Next, mark a 385mm length on the face of it using a pencil and square.

17 Turn the piece on its side and use the square and pencil to extend the line around onto the edge.

18 Press a utility knife straight down on the mark at the corner, along the line, to make an incision.

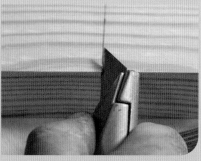

19 Now press the blade in at an angle to make a tiny notch, making sure that it points away from the length of wood you want to keep (i.e. the notch is made in the part of the wood you will cut away).

USING THE WORKBENCH FOR CUTTING

You can use the step in the workbench for making small cuts to length.

20 Clamp the length of yellow pine to your workbench, with the line you just marked hovering over the plane track. Using the small crosscut saw, place the blade carefully in the notch you have cut and hold it at about 10–15° off horizontal.

21 Keep everything steady with your other hand (or add another clamp) and gently but positively begin to cut. Concentrate on the top line. As the cut down the side develops, angle the saw back a bit more to focus on that.

22 The sound the saw makes will get higher in pitch as you near the end of the cut. This is your signal to slow down and do the last couple of strokes much more slowly, in order to avoid breaking the last few fibres or slamming the saw into the bench.

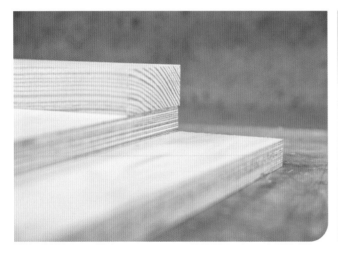 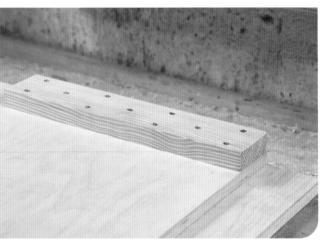

23 Place the length of pine at the back of the board, fractionally overhanging the edge of the plane track.

24 Follow steps 11–13 to drill and countersink the planing stop, using the 4 × 40mm screws. Use the square to line it up, then drive in a couple of screws. Test that the stop is in the right place with the plane; giving a square edge. If the edge is not square, undo a few of the screws and tweak the stop into position. You can adjust the position by slightly undoing a screw to allow movement. Once in place, drive in the centre screws to hold the new position, then drive in the others to fix it in place. If you simply withdraw and then redraw a screw that has already made a hole for itself, you'll find the stop will just be pulled into the same place as before.

Why the overhang?

If you leave the end of the planing stop overhanging by 0.5mm you can plane it perfectly square and flat and in line with the edge of the planing track with your plane.

Why offset screws?

You can add strength through the way you position your screws. I have alternated between having one and two screws, because if you have too many screws along the same line of the grain, they can cause it to split. The reason I spaced the screws further in from the end than the edge is also to prevent splitting.

Getting things square

The final test is whether your plane can cut the end of a piece of wood square. A bigger engineer's square makes it easier to tell what's going on, though here I've just used a 100mm square to set up the stop and got good results anyway. I prefer to adjust the planing stop as described in step 24, rather than planing it while it is fixed in place using a shoulder plane, though either method works. As a finishing touch, I like to cut away the back corner of the planing stop with a chisel to stop it breaking as the plane goes past.

25 Add the front stop. This is smaller than the planing stop and is also adjustable. Its function is for sawing and chiselling against (see 'Stops', right). Cut a 200 × 40mm piece of pine, and screw it into place 100mm from the front of the hook.

Stops

The small stops are intended for sawing and chiselling and can be moved around by simply screwing them in a new position. You might move the stop closer to the front edge if you are working on small components, so that your hand doesn't hit the edge of the workbench, for example.

You can use the edge of the stop to guide your saw when cutting an end square.

The front stop gives you something to hold the wood against as you pare it with the chisel, acting as a backstop which catches the chisel if you cut all the way across the piece. Never use your planing stop to chisel against as this will make the surface rough and lead to inaccuracy.

Stops can be made taller or thinner for different purposes, such as holding thin pieces of wood for planing. They can wear out with time but can just be replaced.

USING THE COPING SAW

A vice is a good addition to your shooting board and enables you to easily hold workpieces in lots of different ways – very useful, particularly when working on the ends. To prevent the metal jaws from marking the wood you are working on, we can make some plywood jaw liners from the offcut left over from step 9.

The interesting thing here is that we need to cut out a section to clear the central screw and guide rods in the middle of the vice. It's a bit long-winded to do this with just a crosscut saw and chisel, but a coping saw will make short work of it. This saw is designed for cutting curves and has a very shallow blade that is replaceable. The blade is held by holders, which rotate so that the frame of the saw can be swung out of the way of the work.

There is limited choice when it comes to coping saws unless you spend quite a bit of money. A basic model like that used here has blade holders that rotate independently in use. This means you can end up with your blade twisted like a spiral and cutting unpredictably or getting jammed. On more fancy coping saws, the blade holders can be locked in position. Make sure you use good quality blades – they are well worth the relatively small investment.

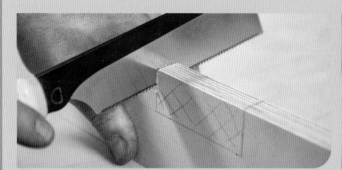

26 Measure your vice and work out how much of the jaws needs to be cut away where the guide rods and screw are. Leave a few millimetres extra clearance around that area. Mark the cut-outs in both pieces with a pencil, ruler and square. The jaws here measure 75mm wide, 200mm long and 18mm thick. It is easier to make these cut-outs and cut to length afterwards. Mark the piece you're cutting out by cross-hatching over it with pencil. Next, saw the end cuts with the small crosscut saw, just inside the pencil marks in the waste wood.

27 Clamp the ply to your workbench with an F-clamp and work the fret saw into the kerf left by the small crosscut saw. About 10mm from the bottom line, start turning the saw into the wood by applying a slight sideways pressure to the saw in the direction you want to go. Make sure to keep the saw blade upright so that it is cutting the same on the top and bottom of the piece.

28 Saw a gentle curve down to the line before following it to the other side. Swing the saw frame out of the way as needed and check that the blade isn't twisted as that can cause it to break.

29 Once you have made the cutouts for each side, you can saw them off the strip of ply. Give your shooting board a try by squaring the ends of the pieces with your plane. Plane away all the corners slightly to remove splinters and then screw the jaws to the vice.

30 Measure and cut two pieces of wood to be stops on the underside of the workbench. These will allow you let it rest against the edge of the table or other support that you are working on – just like a standard bench hook. Because we have added a vice, these pieces also serve to stop the ends of the vice screw and support bars mangling the edge of whatever surface you are resting your workbench on. Wind the vice fully closed and then allow 3mm beyond that point – this ensures that the edge of the pieces are further back than the ends of the vice screw. Drill and screw the stops into position just as before to finish.

HOOK

This project will show you how to saw accurately as well as introducing you to the fascinating technique of steam bending. You'll need a workbench – so if you've made the previous project, this is the perfect opportunity to try it out.

You can cut the blank for the hook from any offcut of suitable sawn hardwood you get your hands on – even a floorboard – but be aware that not all woods will bend as easily as others – some don't bend at all. Beech, ash, oak, walnut, cherry and other fruit woods will all work well for steam bending. I'm using walnut for my hook. There are several other types of wood that will bend – in fact, you are more likely to come across ones that will bend than won't. So, if you have something that you think would be nice to use, then it might be worth having a go and seeing what happens. Avoid any pieces with defects such as knots and grain that runs out to the side.

You will need

— 20mm thick offcut of hardwood
— Scrap wood, such as yellow pine or spruce
— Bench hook and vice
— Saws: small *dozuki* with universal toothing, large *kataba* rip saw
— Marking gauge
— Sliding bevel
— Pencil and ruler
— Engineer's square
— Utility knife
— Twine/string
— 25mm chisel
— Abrasive paper, 120, 180 and 240 grit
— Osmo wax oil
— Cordless drill with 4mm dowel point bit and countersink bit
— Brass screws
— Small ratchet clamp

MEASURING AND MARKING:
USING THE MARKING GAUGE

A marking gauge is used to mark a line parallel to the edge of wood along the grain. I have other, more fancy, marking gauges but I still like this very basic kind as it leaves a nice clear mark. If used across the grain, a marking gauge will tear the fibres, so a different type – a cutting gauge – is used for this purpose. A cutting gauge has a blade rather than a pin.

The technique for setting the gauge to an exact size is this: undo the screw and move the head along the bar to the required measurement. Lightly tighten the screw to hold the head in an approximate position, then tap the end of the gauge on the bench to make any fine adjustments before tightening the screw more securely.

The trick to marking a line with a gauge is to lean it towards the direction of travel and apply mainly lateral pressure. I like to mark an initial very faint line first and then go over it again to make it bolder. This gets the line in the right place without the pin being drawn along the lines of the grain. It is a good idea to practise this – if the lines you mark are wrong, then the cuts you make will be wrong too.

1 Set your marking gauge to 15mm.

2 Angle the gauge away from you and run it down to the end of your offcut of wood, scoring a mark as shown.

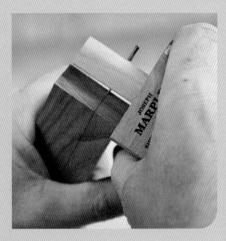

3 Turn the wood and continue the mark over the end.

4 Repeat on the back, drawing the gauge round in a continuous line.

5 Use an engineer's square and pencil to mark a straight line at the end. It doesn't matter if the end of the wood is square or not, as it will be cut away later.

6 Measure 95mm down from the line and mark it with the pencil.

7 Use the square to draw an accurate line across the wood.

MEASURING AND MARKING: USING THE SLIDING BEVEL

The sliding bevel or bevel gauge has many uses. It can be adjusted to match an existing angle within a project, or can be set to the desired angle by using a bevel board for maximum accuracy (a small protractor will work too, but will not be as accurate). To make small adjustments to the setting, I tap the end of the blade on a scrap piece of wood, a bit like finely adjusting a marking gauge. The blade can slide through and sit equally either side of the stock which gives you a positive and negative reading of the same angle from square.

8 Use a bevel board or protractor to set your sliding bevel to 14°, then use the pencil to mark the angle on both sides of the offcut as shown.

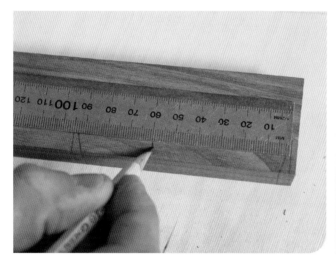

9 Mark a point on the side in between the two marks, 60mm down from the end. This is the length of the slot.

10 Set the marking gauge to 4mm and run it from the pencil marks to the end, over the top and round to mark the slot.

11 Secure the wood in your vice at a gentle angle, then make a start notch with the utility knife (see page 53) on the 15mm line. The angled side of the notch should be in the waste wood, so that the piece you saw remains at 15mm thickness. This cut liberates the hook blank from the rest of the timber.

12 Cut to the waste wood side of the 15mm line with the rip saw. This will become the back of the hook. Cut until you are diagonally just over halfway through, and the saw cut is starting to appear on the underside.

13 Take the wood out of the vice, turn it over and replace it in the vice. Note the kerf you made from the other side.

14 Drop the saw into the kerf: this will guide you to the correct position. Cut down to the marked line on this side.

15 Angle the saw and continue to level off and complete the cut.

16 Repeat the process to saw the 60mm long line that will separate the tip of the hook from the body. This time, cut your start notch with the square side on the 4mm thick side, and the angled notch in the body side of the hook, to maintain the 4mm thickness.

17 To test that the end of the slot is flat, hold the saw in place as shown and check it is in line with the lines on both sides. If this is not flat, the hook will not be straight.

18 Use the small crosscut saw (*dozuki*) to cut along the diagonal lines at top and bottom

19 Lift out the basic blank of the hook. Keeping the hook blank attached to the larger piece of wood up to this point makes it much easier to hold and saw.

Tip

Note the smooth surface created by using the *dozuki*. Japanese crosscut teeth have an extra bevel filed on them which makes the teeth much more knife-shaped than Western crosscut saws. This allows them to cut more finely, each tooth slicing perfectly like a tiny knife blade. With the very finest saws, the surface is left almost perfectly smooth.

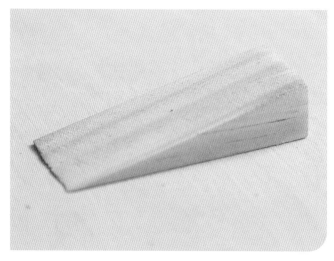

20 Cut a 15° wedge from your scrap wood, measuring 50mm long and 12mm tall at the wide end. Make sure it is even.

21 Tie a length of twine around the hook blank so that you can retrieve it from the water in the next step.

22 Immerse the hook blank in boiling water for five minutes, then, being careful of the heat (you might choose to wear protective gloves, but I never do as I find them cumbersome), use the string to retrieve the blank and immediately force the wedge in until it is just proud of the edge. Support the bottom of the hook with your thumb, as shown, in order to stop it splitting any further. Use a small ratchet clamp to hold it while the wood dries.

23 Wrap the string firmly around to bind the wedge in place, then leave the piece to cool and dry completely – ideally overnight – before removing the wedge.

USING THE CHISEL

The chisel is used here to carve away the waste wood in thin shavings. Pay attention to the direction of the grain, and use a paring grip (see right) for maximum control. Don't be tempted to take too much off at once. It's best to start cautiously.

The paring grip

Paring the wood – that is, cutting it away in layers – requires a lot of control. The trick to keeping accuracy is to cut fine layers down to the line, keeping the surface you are cutting at the same angle as the line you are aiming for.

The left hand is very important for control and for safety. Where your left hand holds the chisel is vital. If you are only cutting a very shallow depth, as here, move your hand right up, close to the cutting edge – your hand will then act as a depth stop.

24 Use a pencil to measure and mark 4mm in from each side of the end of the hook, and draw down to the end of the slot as shown.

25 Place the hook sideways on in your vice, being careful only to grip the lower part, and use the 25mm chisel to begin to pare down to the lines. Work gradually – you can always take more off, but you can't put it back!

26 Once you have worked down to the line on one side, turn the piece in your vice and shave down the other side with the chisel.

27 Drill and countersink two 4mm holes, one 10mm in from the end, and the other 25mm in. Use 180 grit, then 240 grit abrasive paper to smooth the surfaces, being careful not to lose definition on the edges. Lightly sand the corners, to remove any roughness. Next, tip a little wax oil into a shallow container then use a folded-up piece of tissue to wipe it over the surface, working it in. Oiling the hook will protect it from dirt and bring out the colour.

28 Let the oil sit for a few minutes, then buff off the excess with more tissue. Do two or three thin coats like this, allowing it to dry between each one. Dispose of oily tissues carefully. The hook can now be fixed to the wall with slotted head brass screws, though be careful as you wind them in, as they break much more easily than steel screws. I suggest using the same size steel screw first.

Tip

A cork block or scrap block of wood can be used to help with the sanding, and is essential for doing the ends. When sanding the corners, use an old piece of worn-out 240 grit paper if possible, as this will cut slowly, for greater control.

Variations of the design. The double hook in the middle is made from cherry, while the one on the left is carved with an intricate facetted design, all done with the chisel.

BOX

This is a box with lots of different potential uses, and can be made from a differently-sized piece of timber, depending on your intention for it. Although we could make a box by intricately joining strips of wood together at the corners, on a small scale it works really well just to hollow out a solid block to form the inside of the box. The design was inspired by a simple picture frame I made in the same way as a teenager.

The square-section timber used here is the same as you will need for brackets for the shelf project later in the book. It's also a common size of machined softwood if that's the only thing you can get hold of.

This project will build on some of the skills you learnt from making the hook. It involves lots more sawing and chiselling, and introduces the use of the mallet. Using a mallet saves energy and is useful for removing waste wood quickly. I'll also show you how to glue things together and introduce a few other tools such as the block plane and flush-cutting saw.

You will need

— Red cedar, planed to 20 × 100 × 180mm
— Length of ash, 44 × 44mm
— Bench hook and vice
— Saws: small *dozuki* with universal toothing, large *kataba* rip saw, *kugihiki* flush-cutting saw
— Square
— Steel ruler
— 400g plastic mallet
— 25mm chisel
— Utility knife
— Pencil
— Wood glue
— Large and small F-clamps
— Block plane
— Masking tape
— Abrasive paper, 120, 180 and 240 grit
— Wax oil: white-tinted Osmo 'raw', and clear matt oil

1 Mark and cut two 170mm lengths of ash, using the large crosscut saw. Make sure to mark the line all the way round, and follow it. Try to get the cuts as accurate as you can (perhaps with a few practice cuts) – while you can correct an imperfect cut later, things will be much easier with straight cuts.

What is bookmatching?

Bookmatching is the process of matching pieces of wood together so that the grain mirrors for decorative effect. This name comes from the technique of matching thin leaves of veneers that are cut sequentially from a log: you simply separate the leaves like you are opening a book to achieve a mirrored grain pattern.

2 Place the two pieces together so they bookmatch. Draw a triangle, or other asymmetrical mark, across both pieces so that they will only align in one way.

3 Measure in 12mm from the end and make a small mark with the knife at that point. Take the ruler away and swap it with the square, then draw a line from the inside top edge of the block to about 6mm from the outside edge. Next, transfer this line around the joining surface and onto the underneath as well. Do the same on both pieces of ash.

4 Set the marking gauge to 6mm and mark on the top and bottom of both pieces, finishing where it meets the 12mm mark. This is the side of the box.

5 Make a series of cuts down to half a millimetre above the bottom line made with the marking gauge. Knife a start notch and then cut to the 12mm lines at each end with the small crosscut saw (*dozuki*). Next, do a series of cuts about 12mm apart along the waste wood using the large crosscut saw. These are made simply to divide up the waste wood so that it can be broken up with the chisel later; there is no need to mark them.

Making even cuts

To help cut evenly down both sides, hold the saw at an angle of about 10–15° and you will hit the line on the front first. Then, keeping your body in the same position, look over to the back edge, level the saw out and finish the cut slowly.

6 Chock the piece against the front stop of your workbench to secure it. Put the tip of the chisel into one of the saw kerfs near the centre, and strike with the mallet to break the waste wood away. Keep your hands clear – it's easy to slip.

USING THE MALLET AND CHISEL

This technique of dividing the waste wood up with the saw works because slicing across the fibres into short pieces makes the wood weak and easy to break: instead of trying to burrow through a solid block, you're taking it apart in detail. The technique can go wrong if the grain of the piece is not completely straight along the length: grain that slopes away to one side will follow its natural structure and not break evenly along the lines you've marked. You can get round this a little by further dividing the waste wood up, which helps to reduce any deviation.

For shallow cut outs, such as those made for hinges and other hardware, the chisel is used to do the dividing cuts, simply driven straight down into the surface and then pared from the side to make it clean. Knowing ways to divide up and split away wood and using your knowledge of its structure to help you out will save lots of time.

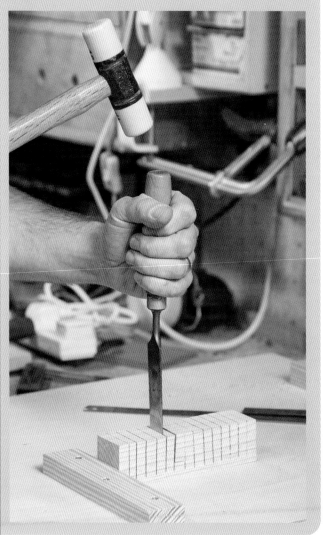

7 Repeat step 6 along the piece, but leave the last piece at each end untouched. Tip out the waste wood.

8 Turn the piece on its side and chisel out the final two pieces as shown. This helps keep control and stops you breaking the ends off the box.

9 Clear off any leftover chunks to get a roughly flat surface. This will be cut back to the 6mm line later, when the piece is easier to hold.

10 Repeat on the other piece, then glue them together as shown, using the wood glue. Make sure the asymmetrical shape matches up.

How much glue should I use?

You need only a thin layer of wood glue – you should be able to see the wood grain through it, as shown.

The glue can act like a temporary lubricant – particularly if you overdo the amount you use – so make sure the pieces don't slide as you apply clamp pressure.

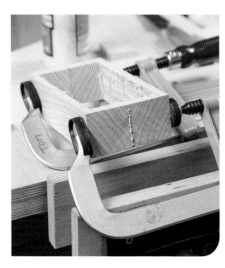

11 Clamp the pieces together and place them to one side to dry. Use scrap wood under your clamp heads if they don't have protective plastic jaws like these.

12 Move the front stop closer to the edge of your workbench as shown, by undoing the screws then redriving them once the stop is in the new position. This will give you enough clearance to use both hands when chiselling in the next step.

13 Clamp the box to the workbench. Hold the chisel with the bevel uppermost in a paring grip (see page 66), then slice down through the waste wood in thin layers until you can locate the chisel in the 6mm marking gauge line and finish the cut. Cutting from both sides alternately will help to keep everything at the same level. Avoid cutting completely across from front to back as you will splinter the back edge. For safety, avoid steadying the box with your hand. You might slip with the chisel and hit yourself – and apart from anything else, you need both hands to control the cut! Use one of your big F-clamps instead.

14 Remove the clamps, turn the piece and, if necessary, clean up any mismatch on the inside where the two sides join.

15 Use the block plane to flatten both surfaces. Set the blade finely and test it on a scrap piece first to check the setting. Plane along the grain with the plane held at an angle as shown to get better reference from the box surface, rather than trying to balance on just one edge at a time.

16 Now for the lid and base parts. These are cut from a piece of 20mm thick red cedar that has machined surfaces that you can measure from to mark the depth. The cedar blank is very easy to cut and also about 20mm overlength and width. Set the marking gauge to 6mm and then run it all around from each side, being careful not to press too hard.

17 Make a start notch with the knife, 1mm away from the 6mm line. This leaves some thickness to plane off later. Using the rip saw, start cutting slowly. Work gradually, cutting diagonally halfway through, then leading the kerf around the blank following the line.

18 Turn the piece in the vice and use the cut at the corner to guide you as you saw the rest of the face off. This will be the lid of the box.

19 Sand the machined surface of the lid down to make it smooth; it's awkward to try to do this later. Use fine 180 and 240 grit abrasive paper as the wood is soft and will cut quickly. A sanding block will help keep it flat. Check that the lid sits flush on the top of the box body.

USING ABRASIVE PAPER

Sanding is all about gradually refining the surface. This is done by using successfully finer grits of paper, each removing the scratches from the previous one until they are too small to see.

Sand along the grain to hide the scratches from the paper amongst the grain pattern. On end grain it doesn't matter which way you sand.

The coarseness of the paper is described as a grit number, which is the number of grit particles in a square inch. The smaller the particles, the more fit in the space, which results in a higher number and finer grit. The roughest grit I use is 80 grit which is mainly for removing material and levelling things (to remove dents, for example). I use 120 grit for general refinement, 180 to refine further, and 240 to gain further clarity to the wood, free from visible scratches. The highest I go to is 500 grit, but this isn't needed for every project. If you've got some 120, 180 and 240, then you are all set. I try to start off sanding with the finest grade that will do the job, so if the surface already looks pretty clean then you might try skipping 120 grit and going straight to 180.

Avoid traditional glasspaper as it will shed grit all over your work – it's rubbish! Instead, buy enough good-quality aluminium oxide paper that you will not be worried about using it up as you wear through it. A cork sanding block to

wrap the paper round will help you keep flat surfaces flat – though I've just been using suitably sized wood offcuts for years.

For detail work, I tear off a rectangular piece of paper (roughly quarter of a sheet) that I then fold into thirds – the paper then has a bit more strength and stops you just wearing a hole in the middle of a sheet, wasting the rest.

On very soft woods, like the cedar used here, be careful not to remove too much material. Finer grades give you more control.

20 Saw out a 20 × 6mm strip of cedar with the rip saw, then square the end off using the plane on the shooting board section of your workbench.

21 Place the length against the box as shown and mark the length you need to fit snugly within the box.

22 Cut a second length and check they fit by placing them within the box. If correctly cut, they should sit securely, as shown. Smear a thin layer of glue onto the pieces. Don't go right up to the edges of the strips – this will ensure the glue doesn't get squeezed out everywhere.

23 Turn over and place the glued side down onto the previously-sanded surface of the lid.

24 Use the pencil to make reference marks to help you align it later.

25 Press the strips down in position inside the box. Let it sit for a minute and then, while holding the strips down, pull the box body off the lid, leaving the strips in place. This will ensure the lid and body are not glued together. This process is easy if done before the bottom is glued on the box, which is why we do it first.

26 Cut another piece of cedar in the same way as you cut the lid earlier (see steps 16–18).

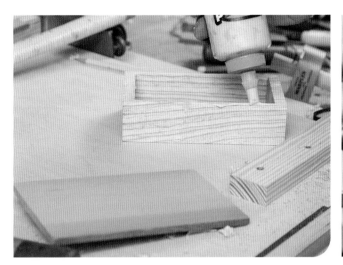

27 Sand down the machined face and then apply glue to the bottom of the box. Leave a small margin on the inside edge to avoid the glue squeezing out into the inside corners.

28 Sandwich the box and lid with spare bits of wood, then use the clamps to hold them together. Allow plenty of time to dry – overnight is best. Be careful not to position the clamps over the empty space inside the box.

29 Remove the clamps and place the lid on top of the box. Holding the plane at an angle, push away from you to flatten the surface. Working at an angle will help you because it eases the blade through the wood. Take only fine shavings. A low-angle block plane is ideal for this.

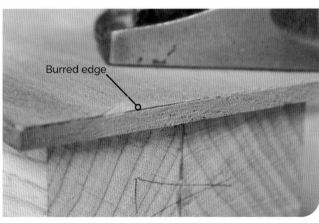

Burred edge

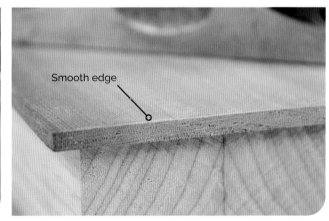

Smooth edge

30 You'll know when you get to the right level, because the edge will be burred – this is the result of the cut made by the gauge. Continue planing until the effect is no longer visible.

31 Use the ruler as a level to check that the surface is flat, then repeat on the bottom surface of the box.

32 Holding it flat against the side of the box, use the flush-cutting saw to trim away the excess cedar overhang across the grain of both bottom and top. Be careful as you finish the cut.

The box, with the cross-grain cuts made.

33 Use the plane to cut with the grain, removing the excess at the sides.

34 Cut two more 6mm strips and glue them on as feet. Make sure you stick them to the base, not the top!

35 Use the flush-cutting saw to trim away the excess, then sand them down.

Why different oils?

The white tinted oil stops the ash looking yellow, but it can't be used on cedar as this wood soaks oil up like a sponge, giving a murky-looking result.

36 Sand down all the surfaces until smooth.

37 Use masking tape to protect the cedar, then use white-tinted oil to finish the ash wood with a cloth. Oil the cedar with clear matt oil.

The finished box.

MOVING ON

In this section we are going to work at a slightly larger scale. The projects include a shelf that is held together with wedges and a chest based on a very old design. If you break these more advanced projects down into processes, you will see that lots of things involved are similar to what you've done before; using fundamental techniques such as cutting to length with the saw and plane, chiselling to a line and marking out with a square and utility knife. Repetition will improve your skill level, and you should aim to make your process slicker and better every time.

I've made some variations of the projects in this section to show you that you can use an idea and develop it into other things. With the shelf project I used the same wedged brackets idea to make a much smaller shelf out of a thin reclaimed oak board (see page 109). I've even used the same technique to make a multiple shelf – that is, a variation with long wall brackets and three shelves of different sizes stacked up. My advice is to make each project as I designed it first, so

you have time to understand it and get some insight into why I made it a certain way. Once you have that under your belt, try making your own variation by adding some flourishes. As your confidence builds, you can let your designs evolve from mine. A simple way to start designing is to alter small details, such as whether the edges are rounded or chamfered, and by how much. These make a surprisingly big difference and can affect the whole feel of a piece.

The finish you choose to apply to protect the wood – varnish, laquer, oil and so forth – can make a big difference too; as can the time you take on finishing. If you only roughly sand your project then coat it with thick glossy varnish, it won't have the same quality as something that has been carefully sanded to a million grit and oiled.

These pages look at fundamentals of design so that you can bear them in mind when you begin the longer projects – and I hope that will set you up to begin experimenting yourself.

DESIGNING YOUR OWN PROJECTS

Have you ever come across an object, furniture or otherwise that just feels 'right'? Perhaps it's an old chair that has carefully shaped arms that feel nice to rest your hands on, or a table that has the legs in just the right places so everyone can fit around it.

Sometimes such results are accidental but usually someone has spent some time thinking about it. Form and function work together and are the cornerstones of good design. It's worth noting that there are certain sizes things should be to feel comfortable – an obvious one is the height of chairs and tables; get either (or both) wrong and you could end up with your feet not touching the ground and a table you can't get your legs under! Something can be well made and technically very proficient, but it may still not be well designed.

HOW DO I DESIGN WELL?

If you are working at home, then how your projects turn out will be a balance between your skill, the function of the piece, the time you have available and the quality of your tools and materials. All of these elements come together to become your design. If one or more of these things is wrong, then things might not turn out as expected.

Give yourself the best chance of success by using good materials: the cost of materials is a small part of the overall project cost when compared with the time spent making it. Buy good tools. They will become trustworthy allies you can rely on and last you a very long time. Finally, don't give yourself too great a challenge: it's meant to be enjoyable, not an epic slog. These fundamental plans will help to set you up for design success.

TAKE YOUR TIME

Time spent refining things in the design stages will save hours of time later. As a result, when designing your own project, it's good to carefully think through how something is put together before starting to make it. You might be committing yourself to cutting unnecessarily difficult joints or using awkwardly sized wood.

As part of the design process, I often make a mock-up of the project from cheap or scrap materials so I can get an idea of how it will look and feel. This can often simply be screwed together. I then make the joint details as separate samples, which lets me test the process of making them and also see how they look.

WHEN IT DOESN'T GO TO PLAN

You might start making a piece of furniture and then realize that there is something fundamental you need to change about it. Perhaps the proportions are wrong or the joinery flawed. This is part of the learning process. Obviously you want to make nice things, but even when it doesn't go to plan, you should feel good that you are a couple of steps further down the road in learning your craft than you would otherwise be.

It's okay to make mistakes. Learn from them and keep going. I've been woodworking for most of my life and the feeling of being on a learning curve never leaves me. That's the whole experience: be open to it.

EXAMPLE DESIGN:
COLLECTOR'S SHELF

I found a drawer in a junk shop that was used to store printing equipment. It has lots of tiny dividers carefully joined into each other. I put it up on the wall to hold small stones, leaves and other treasures that we have found on days out. Eventually, I started thinking about a version that could be made to fit specific objects – collections of things like stones and shells collected on the beach, for example, or badges, toy cars or figures. The design would also work to show off other everyday objects that might look nice on display, like colourful nail varnish bottles, jewellery or stationery.

I want you to think about all these things and design a simple set of collector's shelves that can be used in your home based on the sort of techniques you can see I've used in mine – though of course you can adapt them to the materials you have.

The inspiration: a printer's type drawer.

ASK SOME QUESTIONS

It's hard not to have a vague idea of how you might make a project already, but spending time thinking about how an object might be used before getting down to the design will help you make decisions later on. The easy mistake you can make is to settle on the first idea that comes to mind – it may be based on assumptions you've made.

Here are the questions I asked myself when forming the idea for the collector's shelf opposite – along with any answers I found, or my notes on further considerations that the questions brought up. You could use this as a prompt when designing your own. With any design, at least some answers are likely to be simple, but it's important to think about even the obvious ones.

Collector's shelf design notes

What is this for? Displaying interesting objects; either so they can be enjoyed simply by looking at them, or to help the user see which thing they need.

Who will use it? Myself or for a loved one.

Will it be located in a humid or arid location? The material choice and finishing need to take this into account.

How big should the sections be, and what will fit in them? I think it would be specific to the situation; though maybe a selection of sizes would be useful – if it's too specific, it will be less functional.

Are the objects displayed in it heavy or very light? If the objects are light, they might be moved by a breeze, they might need some means of holding them down: anything really heavy probably won't fit anyway.

How long have I got to make it? This is relative to each person that makes it, but it should be a quick project so that different types can be made to try out different ideas without a big investment of time.

How will it fix to the wall? It will simply hang on a screw or two.

How else might someone use or misuse it? It might be used it as a tray instead of being wall-mounted.

What techniques can I use? Very basic glued-together construction, reinforced with a backing to give it strength, might work; or with thin wood, small cross-halving joints could be cut.

Have I got appropriately-sized wood available or ready-cut? If so, I should consider adapting the design to use this, rather than buying new wood.

What wood would be technically best? Since it will hang on just a screw or two, it might be best made from lightweight wood like cedar or mid-weight wood like beech or ash.

What wood would be most beautiful to use? I like walnut – that's an easy answer. However, perhaps this wood will draw too much attention, and something lighter would be better?.

What finish will it have? It's not going to be handled much, so the strength of the finish is not crucial, as long as it can be dusted and cleaned easily. Oil, wax oil, wax or shellac would be fine.

What about wood movement? If it is too wide or thin, it may bow or twist. Keeping the dividers quite small will help to avoid this problem.

The finished collector's shelf

Looking at what I've made here will help you start to generate your own ideas about what to make. Be sure to really evaluate your design before starting, ask yourself questions about it and refine it down.

EXAMPLE DESIGN: TABLE

Here is a small side table I made for my home. I wanted something small enough to fit near the sofa without getting in the way. I also wanted to keep the structure of it lightweight. There's no need to waste wood by making it super-chunky, as it just doesn't need that sort of heft: I only want to put a couple of plants and maybe a cup of coffee on it. It's made using the same tools as in the rest of this book but with more advanced joinery (see pages 88–89).

DESIGN NOTES

As you can see from the image of the timber (right), there's not a lot of wood needed – big thick legs were not required, and neither was a very heavy underframe. When designing, think about what forces each piece needs to resist. Here, everything could be thin as it is in tension or compression, with not much racking or side loads to worry about; as there would be with a chair, for example. The table legs are just 15mm thick but are 35mm wide – the width gives a good contact surface at the joint and stops the table from wobbling.

I sized the table to be lower than the seating height of a normal chair; partly to discourage anyone from sitting on it and also because the slim legs then look in proportion to the top. The batten underneath the top is sized to have enough heft to it that it can keep the top flat and stop the top breaking. It is tapered towards the ends in both directions so that it is hard to see unless you view from below the level of the top. The batten is fixed on with heavy brass screws, through holes that are opened out to 10mm on the inside. This allows the top to expand and contract and allows the screws to flex rather than breaking themselves or splitting the top.

I drew the joint in my sketchbook at full size to help decide on the best way of working: it's easier to work through some things on paper first, as there are often details that aren't apparent whilst just imagining it. I also made a full size mock-up of the top-to-leg sliding dovetail joint and the underframe wedged joint (see right). It's good to make this out of the same wood as you will use for the final object if possible. That way you get used to how best to cut the same wood before you start the real thing. It also gives you a chance to refine the design – you might notice that the final joints are slightly different from the mock-up.

Timber sizes:

Seeing all the components cut to size underlines how little wood is needed. For the tabletop itself, I used: two 490 × 245 × 20mm pieces of Douglas fir. Offcuts of this were used for the wedges. The legs are made from four 380 × 35 × 15mm lengths of beech, and the underframe from two 495 × 20 × 15mm pieces.

Design sketch and joint mock-ups

All of the components that make the joint itself are produced at full scale: note the pieces of the wedged joint shown below match the size shown in the sketch. This helps to ensure that the materials work correctly together. Note, however, that only a section of the table top was mocked-up (bottom) – there's no need to test this, so you can save yourself a bit of wood.

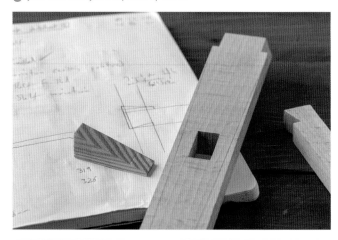

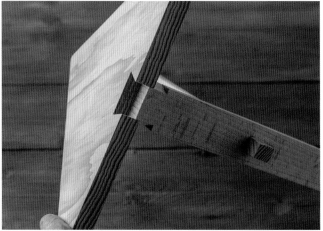

The finished table

USING THE DESIGN: NOTES ABOUT MAKING

The leg to underframe joint works like this: the mortise (see page 89) through the leg is angled at the top and bottom. The angle here is then used to mark out the wedge and to cut a half dovetail on the lower edge of the tenon. The way to get them fitting perfectly is to hollow the internal surfaces by a tiny fraction so that the outside edges are in full contact.

To mark the sliding dovetail cutout in the top, start by cutting the dovetail into the top of the leg; then, making sure the sides are dead square, measuring down from the top end of the leg. If you clamp another piece of wood to the top, along the outside of the line on which the corresponding cutout is to be made, you can butt the leg up against it as you mark round it with the knife. Each one will be individual, so number them as you go.

The top is made from Douglas fir which is renowned for its stability. I started with a board a bit more than twice as long as the top and then cut it and matched the grain edge to edge. As a result, the grain flows together nicely. I chose a board which, when looked at from the end, had growth rings running from left to right. This makes it look like there is no end grain on the top, which is something I think looks good here. All the beech for the legs is quarter-sawn (see page 14) so it has a fine fleck of medullary rays on the surface. Without this, chiselling it might look a bit boring.

Details of the underframe wedged joint

The pictures here show how the angled mortise joint slots in neatly (above left), before the decorative wedge is pushed into place (above right). Once fully assembled (right), the wedge is trimmed down flush with the underframe, which projects slightly.

Tried and tested

It's good to think about how someone might misuse the table so I tested the finished piece by standing on top of it – not that I expect it to be used that way, but it's good to know that the design is strong enough to cope.

DESIGN AND INSPIRATION

Before designing the octagonal table with a wedged underframe seen on page 85, I developed the round one shown here, which features a steam-bent underframe.

The shape of the octagonal table was inspired by the layout lines I drew on to mark the joint positions for the round table shown here. It just goes to show that inspiration can strike from anywhere, so follow your curiosity.

JOINTS

The purpose of cutting woodworking joints is to lock the surfaces together and provide some mechanical interaction. Most joints are glued together for good measure. In the past, glues weren't as good, so joints that rely more on mechanical interlocking of the wood were essential.

Having made the projects so far in this book, you will have built up a good base of knowledge. From this, you can start to extend your skills, by trying out some of these joints.

HALVING JOINT

Half of each component is cut away so that they lock together. The fit needs to be good or the joint will be weak. Halving joints can be used for making frames of various scales.

This is the joint I used to join the underframe of the octagonal table on page 85. The trick to an accurate fit is to mark the joint size directly from the other piece of wood itself, rather than measuring it.

T-HALVING JOINT

Useful for adding a cross-member in a long frame, as shown above; this type of joint can also be used as a corner joint. When cutting, make sure you cut halfway through on each side, so that each part is equally strong. The depth to cut in each piece should be marked with the marking gauge.

MORTISE AND TENON: THROUGH, WITH WEDGES

A. The mortise is the hole shaped to hold the tenon.

B. The tenon is a projecting piece. Here, cuts have been made to create gaps.

For this type of joint, the hole is made all the way through the wood. The wedges are driven into saw cuts made in the tenon before it is assembled. Once the wedges are driven in, the tenon is expanded by them and can't come apart.

Mortise and tenon joints are typically used to make any sort of doors, attach table legs, build a house – in fact, anywhere where strength is important, or you need a really reliable joint. They can also be used at a very small scale. When measuring, divide the wood into thirds to make sure the wood on either side of the mortise is equally strong.

MORTISE AND TENON: STOPPED

Stopped mortise and tenon joints are slightly easier to make than a through mortise and tenon (see above) because less of the joint is on show – any little mistakes or chipped edges get hidden. This type of joint relies on glue, but it can have a dowel driven through it after the glue has dried. This will stop it falling apart if the glue fails in the future.

BRIDLE JOINT

Sometimes also called an open mortise and tenon, a bridle joint is useful on exposed corners where maximum strength is needed, such as the junction between the front leg and side rail of a chair. This is a pretty joint and represents a halfway house between a halving joint and a mortise and tenon. Bridle joints are easy to cut if you use a marking gauge with two pins, commonly called a mortise marking gauge. This will ensure each piece is marked consistently with the other.

DOVETAIL JOINT

For some, this joint represents the pinnacle of woodworking skill. An excellent joint for making cabinets and drawers, dovetail joings will survive the test of time and look beautiful too. The shape resists pulling forces very well, which is why they have always been a favourite for drawers. They can be time-consuming to cut in long runs (widths) and can look a bit showy, but it's usually worth the effort.

BOX JOINT

A type of joint often used on old wooden packing crates, the large number of interlocking surfaces provides a very large surface area for glue and helps to make this joint very strong. I use them to make small trays and keepsake boxes. Because of the precision required, box joints are often cut by machine. If you don't have a router table and table saw used along with a jig to cut these, you will likely have a much better time cutting dovetails (see opposite).

COMBINING JOINTS

I consider different types of joints as ingredients in a recipe – you can use a few of them mixed together. Here I have taken a simple rebate (US: rabbet) joint, which is a step along an edge or end of a board, and mixed in the idea of mortise and tenon joinery to make a tiny triple tenon joint, or rebated triple mortise and tenon. Some of my inspiration was from larger intricate Japanese woodwork.

DECORATIVE SHELF

It's time to make something slightly bigger than the projects we started with. Making this shelf will give you the opportunity to develop the skills you have learnt so far. We focus on the joints between the shelf and brackets: accurate marking and cutting with the saw and chisel is needed to make sure the shelf sits square.

There's a lot of chisel work, including simple shaping, that will develop your affinity for this simple-looking tool – remember that the complicated and subtle part is how you use it. Practice is essential.

The shelf is held in place with a walnut wedge which is extremely strong as long as everything fits properly. The joint in the bracket is forgiving to make, too. If you spoil the cutting of the edges you can simply re-mark it and try again, then cut a bigger wedge to take up the slack.

Cutting the angle on the ends of the blocks is good practice for cutting the joint itself, because the same angle is used there as on the angled cutout and wedge. The brackets need to be thick enough to be strong, but could be shaped further if you make another shelf later on.

You will need

— 44 × 44mm length of ash
— 1,000 × 140 × 20mm piece of ash
— 20mm thick offcut of walnut
— Sliding bevel
— Saws: large *kataba* crosscut saw, small *dozuki* crosscut saw, large *kataba* rip saw
— Chisels: 25mm and 12mm
— 400g plastic mallet
— Bench plane and block plane
— Utility knife
— Cordless drill, 5mm and 10mm dowel point drill bit
— Sanding block and abrasive paper, 120, 150 and 240 grit
— Wax oil: white-tinted Osmo 'raw', and clear matt oil
— Rasp and file (optional)

Standard sizes

A detail that I hope makes life easier is that I've made the shelf bracket wood the same dimensions as that used for the previous box project.

The shelf and chest use the same size ash boards, too, so you can order a few boards machined to the right width and thickness. Use the best bits for the chest and any oddball pieces, such as those with wilder grain, for the shelf.

MAKING AND MARKING UP THE BRACKETS

A good shelf relies on accuracy. The wood we're using for the shelf itself is 20mm thick, so we need to create brackets that have a gap of slightly more than that – the difference will leave a small gap that we then account for with our decorative walnut wedges.

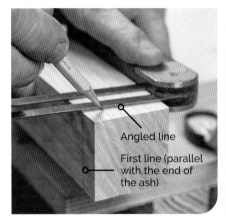

Angled line

First line (parallel with the end of the ash)

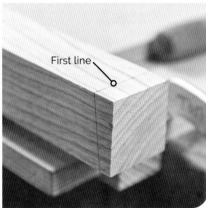

First line

1 Draw a line slightly in from the end of the 44 × 44mm length of ash, parallel with the end itself. Turn the piece 90°, set the sliding bevel to 8° and mark an angled line that meets the first line.

2 Follow the line round the other two faces of the ash, so you end up with two angled lines and two straight lines. Turn the ash so that the first line is uppermost, as shown. This is the front face of the bracket.

3 Make a mark 145mm down from the first line, then draw a line across at the mark, parallel with the first line.

Parallel lines

Front face

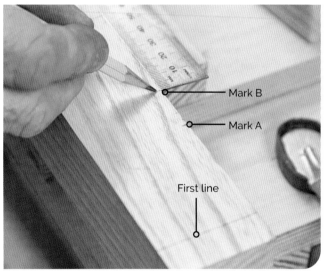

Mark B

Mark A

First line

4 Turn the length of ash so the front face is facing forward, then follow the line around (see steps 1 and 2). Use the sliding bevel set at 8° to draw the angled lines, and note that the angles should mirror those at the other end, not be parallel with them.

5 Turn the ash so the front face is uppermost, then mark 60mm in from each of the parallel lines on this face, leaving a gap between marks A and B (see above) of 25mm. This is the cut-out for the shelf itself, so if the width of the wood you're using for your shelf is different, you'll need to adjust the gap.

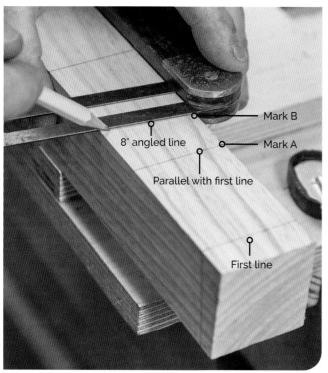

Mark B

8° angled line

Mark A

Parallel with first line

First line

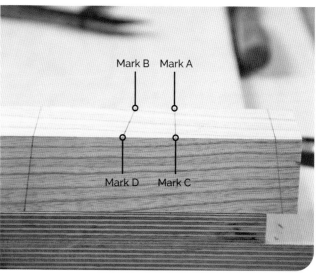

A shot from the side for clarity, showing the various lines. The front face of the piece is facing upwards. Mark C is at the end of the line from A, while D is at the end of the angled line from B.

Mark B Mark A

Mark D Mark C

6 Draw a line parallel with the first line from mark A, and a line at an 8° angle from mark B. The angled line is to allow a space for the wedge to fit into.

7 Turning the piece as necessary, use the square and pencil to mark parallel lines on the sides of the ash, extending from marks A, B, C and D.

8 Set your marking gauge to 20mm and mark between the two sets of new lines on the side faces. The gauge head is running on the front surface of the bracket.

9 Use the pencil to indicate the area to be cut away.

10 Use the large crosscut saw to cut off the end of the ash. You may find it helpful to get down to eye level to make sure your cut is straight.

11 Place the ash face upwards, then notch it with a knife to make a starting point for the saw.

Mark the waste

Note that I'm making the notches in the ash in the waste side – this ensures that the saw kerf is in the waste area.

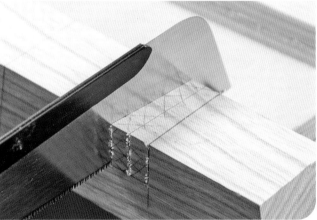

12 Use the small crosscut saw to cut down to the mark.

13 Repeat on the other side, then make some additional cuts within the waste.

Tip

When clearing the waste, remember to keep the flat side of the chisel against the side you want to keep clean.

14 Use the 25mm chisel and mallet to break up the waste. This is a similar technique to that used for the box (see 'Using the mallet and chisel' on page 71).

15 Use the 12mm chisel to clear out the waste. Trim any inaccuracy away from the sides with the chisel. Mark new lines, if necessary, using the knife so that the chisel edge can pick up on them easily.

16 Use the large crosscut saw to cut the piece away.

17 Secure the piece in your vice and use the block plane to clean the ends. Be careful not to plane across the back edge, as it will splinter.

18 Holding the plane at 45° to the block as shown, prepare to chamfer the corners.

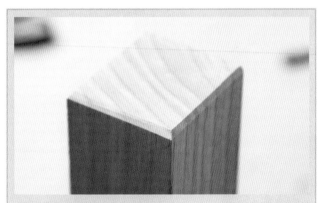

What is a chamfer?

Chamfered edges are symmetrical slopes on the corners or sides of a piece, as shown – in this example, they are all at 45°. A chamfer is a good base for a rounded edge, as it is easier to see if it is consistent.

When creating a chamfer, count the number of times you plane the first corner, then repeat for consistency in depth as well as angle.

19 Chamfer the front and side faces, but not the back, and not the shelf slot.

USING THE DRILL

A cordless drill is quite safe but there are some safety rules to follow. Never drill towards your hands or body. You can unthinkingly get into a position where this is possible, or the drill can advance through the wood quicker than expected. Keep in mind the question 'what will happen if?'. Keep all loose clothing and hair away from the drill as it can easily get tangled. Finally, don't get complacent once you are used to the drill: make sure you keep hold of whatever you are drilling.

When marking out positions for holes, screws or dowels mark the centre of each hole with a small cross showing distance from the edge and spacing along that distance from the edge. Make a small divot with an awl on each point which will help the drill start in the right place.

Avoid driving screws right at the end or very near the edges of a piece of wood as they can split it easily at that point. I don't always drill a pilot hole, but if I do I will make it the size of the central core of the screw (you can measure this size with a vernier caliper). One reason for not drilling a pilot hole is that undrilled wood compresses more around the screw, giving a better fixing. Note that this technique can't be used in all woods – oak, for example, is too dense, and usually the screws aren't going in very deeply anyway, making a pilot hole unnecessary.

Be careful of splintering when drilling all the way through something as this can be severe , especially with blunt or poor-quality bits. You should drill through into a piece of scrap to avoid splintering on the other side of the piece.

20 Round over the chamfered edges with the plane, by taking the corners off each one. Doing it like this helps to keep the curves consistent. Once all the edges are rounded, make two marks, one 20mm down from the top, the other 15mm down from the top of the slot.

21 As you start drilling, think about which direction to look at the drill to see if it's at the right angle. Drill the top hole out with a 10mm bit, at least 15mm deep. Change to a 5mm bit to drill through to the other side.

22 Countersink the lower hole, then sand the surfaces to finish the bracket.

23 Make a second bracket in the same way, mirroring the angles for the cut-out section (i.e. the line between marks B and D runs in the other direction).

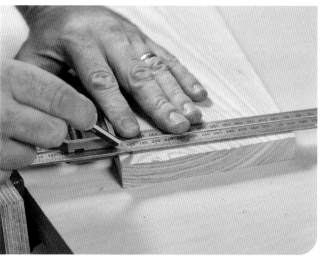

24 Square off the shelf (the 140 × 20mm piece of ash) to tidy the ends. You can cut as much or as little as you like, in order to get the shelf the correct length for your use. Use the square to get your line accurate.

25 Change to the small crosscut saw for the cut.

26 Brace the shelf against the stop and use the bench plane to plane both ends smooth. Note the grip I'm using on the plane. This keeps the blade pressed against the work.

What are machining marks?

Machining marks are the subtle wave-like shapes created by the rotary cutter used to mill the piece of wood. They need to be removed with a plane for a professional finish to your shelf.

When planing, look to keep the shavings as wide as the shelf itself, as shown above. This shows you're taking wood off the whole of the surface and helps to make sure you are keeping the edge square.

27 Put the shelf in the vice and plane along the length to remove the machining marks. Set the plane to get very fine shavings, and look at the grain carefully beforehand, to decide which way to plane.

28 Draw round a circular object to get a curve on the front corners. Here I'm using the base of a glue bottle.

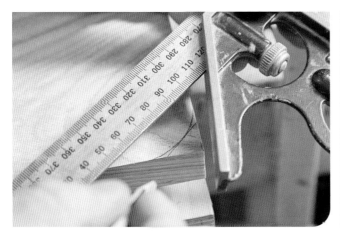

29 Use the square to draw a line at 45° across the apex of the curve.

30 Use the small crosscut saw to cut the corner away.

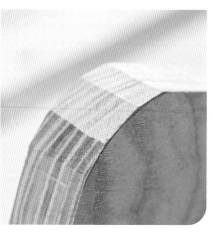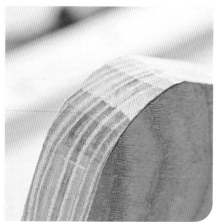

31 Put the shelf in the vice and use the 25mm chisel at an angle to shear away the excess and create facets on the corner. In these pictures, the end of the shelf is to the left.

32 Round off the corner further by chiselling between the facets.

Another approach

A rasp and file can be used to round off the corners, if you prefer. Draw these tools along, rather than across, the grain, to avoid tearing.

33 Sand the corner smooth using the sanding block and 120 grit abrasive paper.

34 Repeat on the other front corner.

35 Place the shelf in the vice, top facing towards you. Measure 75mm in from the corner, and use the knife to make a mark.

36 Align the bracket to the mark and use the knife to mark the other side. Using the bracket itself, rather than an abstract measure, ensures accuracy.

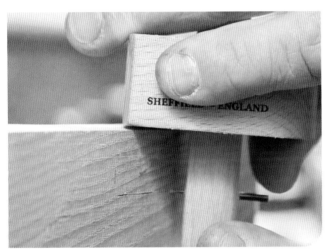

37 Use the pencil to make rough marks on the top surface that align with the knife marks, then set the marking gauge to 20mm and run between them. Repeat on the other side (the back surface).

38 Make the two vertical cuts with the small crosscut saw. Start at a 45° angle to work down to the mark, then gradually flatten out the angle to ensure clean cuts. Make additional cuts within the waste wood.

39 Use the mallet and chisel to remove the waste wood.

40 Clean up the surface with the chisel.

41 Use the engineer's square to check the area is level and square.

42 Test-fit the bracket. It should extend 5mm beyond the back of the shelf. This will account for any unevenness in the wall to which the shelf is secured. If it doesn't fit, then check the cut out in the shelf for accuracy, and carefully chisel or file as needed.

43 Cut the other bracket joint in the same way, then use the block plane to round off all the edges of the shelf, except for the joint faces.

44 Set the sliding bevel to 8° and mark a line on your walnut offcut, 2mm in from the corner.

45 Use the large rip saw to cut the basic shape of the wedge.

46 Clean up the cut edge with the block plane.

47 Test-fit the bracket, tapping it in with the mallet. It should extend slightly beyond the bracket, as shown. Measure the distance it stands proud and mark that distance on the wide end.

48 Cut to length with the small crosscut saw, then chamfer and round the edges using the 12mm chisel.

49 Tap the finished wedge into place with the mallet.

50 Make another wedge for the other side in the same way, then sand all the pieces thoroughly. Oil the wedges, shelf and shelf brackets separately.

MAKING THE PEGS

These pegs are added, first and foremost, to cover over and disguise the screw heads; but it's worth bearing in mind that there's no reason such functional elements can't also be beautiful and decorative. Being so small, they're an ideal way to use up beautiful offcuts that might otherwise go to waste. Using pieces of the same wood we used for the wedges helps the design to hang together.

51 Cut a small (12–15mm) piece from your offcut of walnut.

52 Use a 10mm lip-and-spur bit to mark the end by pressing the point into the centre and lifting away. Note that it leaves a central divot surrounded by a small, neat circle.

What is a lip-and-spur bit?

A lip-and-spur (or dowel point) bit is a clean-cutting type of drill bit that has several advantages over a standard twist drill. A central lead point allows you to place the drill exactly on a mark and stops it wandering. The spur cuts a circle into the wood which is then removed by the cutting edge. This prevents splintering and gives perfect results. I use drills made by Fisch which cut beautifully.

53 Use a utility knife to whittle it down to the circular outer mark, shaping the peg.

54 Use the block plane to further taper the peg.

55 Place the peg in the screw hole to check the fit.

56 Cut the peg down to 25mm in length using the small crosscut saw.

57 Once the shelf is screwed to the wall (see 'Mounting the shelf'), use the mallet to knock the peg into the hole securely.

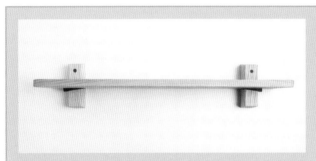

Mounting the shelf

Wedge the shelf into the wall brackets securely. Next, hold it in the position you want it to be on the wall, and use a spirit level on the top surface to align it. Then get an assistant to run a cheap or worn-out 5mm drill through the top holes to mark the wall behind: this will mark the soft plaster surface easily. Do not use your good drill bits for this or they will be ruined.

Move the shelf away and drill for appropriate 8mm wall plugs. Disassemble the shelf and screw the brackets to the wall with 5mm diameter screws, making sure the screws are long enough to expand the plug along its whole length. Try the shelf in place to check the alignment of the brackets before carefully removing it and marking the holes in the bottom of the cutouts in the brackets with the drill like before.

Undo the screws slightly to allow the brackets to rotate out of the way and then drill the points you marked with 8mm holes for wall plugs. Rotate the brackets back and drive the last two screws in, then tighten up the first two. Put the shelf in place and drive the wedges in. If everything looks right and sits level, then add the plugs that cover the top screws and use the flush-cut saw to trim them off (see step 58, right). If the brackets don't quite line up then you can try adjusting their position a bit with the small mallet.

58 To finish, use a flush-cut saw to trim the pegs down for a perfect finish.

The finished shelf.

This variation on the shelf is much smaller and narrower. Made from oak and walnut, instead of ash, it is otherwise made in the same way.

Varying the design

From the basic design you can experiment with variations. Scaled-down versions work really well, as do ones with extended brackets with multiple shelf levels. Be aware of what effect changing the dimensions will have. Increasing the length of the shelf, for example, is not too much trouble; but a wider shelf can bear much less weight. Doubling the width will take it beyond the capabilities of the design, and loading such a shelf with heavy books will likely cause it to collapse. The design here works because the width of the shelf restricts how much can be put on it – and where.

CHEST

The six-board chest is a very old design that gets its name from the number of boards used to make it – four sides, plus the top and bottom. Traditionally, it is made from wide boards, split from as large a log as can be found and easily worked, so that there are as few joins as possible. My version uses paired boards of identical width, which are glued together to form the sides, top and bottom. The pieces are the same width as used for the shelf project (see pages 92–109). The finished chest will do double duty as a seat and for storage. I have one at home by a piano – not that I can actually play it! – and use it to store sheet music.

Sometimes you become acutely aware of all the craftspeople that have gone before you and refined a design, trying different ways of doing things and then keeping the ways that work. It is a good idea to accept this knowledge and learn from it; but remember that you are also part of this chain of development. Here, I have followed the general outline of a traditional chest in the way the sides and ends are jointed together, but I've used dowels instead of mortise and tenons and nails to make the project more approachable – useful if it's the first big thing you've made. I have kept all the joints square, where on a traditional chest the sides are angled in toward the top. Again, this is mainly for simplicity, but on a practical note, it also gives extra space inside.

The dowel jointing used here is not as heavy-duty as the traditional method but it better suits our set-up, and the way the sides and ends are joined still gives the piece lots of strength. Make sure that all your pieces fit together well: the ends must be square in both directions. Any ill-fitting pieces can compromise the strength of the simple joinery by allowing movement that gradually works the joints apart.

If you are careful with planning which bit goes where, you will be able to get nice grain matches where boards are glued together so they look like they are one piece. This sort of detail lends a more refined feel to any project. I've allowed extra material so you have some room to select the best bits.

Variations

It is possible to scale the chest up by using wider boards, though I wouldn't try this with the first one you make. The wider the boards are, the more critical good timber selection is – Using quarter-sawn timber is a very good idea. With narrower boards, timber selection is still important but the effect of the wood cupping across the width will be much less significant.

As a variation you might try making the top from a different wood, although I would stick with one species for the rest of the chest for the sake of stability. An easy way to change the finished chest is through shaping the lid. You might try a roundover or a chamfer of different size – think about how it will feel in use.

PREPARING THE PANELS

1 We start by making the long side panels. Measure in 25mm or so from the end of the board to avoid any splits or grit on the end. Mark a line square across the face of the board with the utility knife. If necessary, use a ruler pressed against the side of the square as shown to give you the extra reach needed for this wide board. Mark another line 560mm from the first in the same way.

Why use the plane?

Using the plane and shooting board ensures that the ends are exactly square. Ensure that your plane is freshly sharpened and also check that the sole is square to the sides.

2 Use the large crosscut saw to cut the board to the outside of these lines, leaving 1mm of so of waste wood (feel free to leave a bit more if you are not yet confident of your sawing). There is a bit of effort involved to do this by hand. If you find it hard, consider getting the pieces cut to length by machine, or do it yourself with a powered mitre saw. Use the shooting board with your bench plane to cut back to the lines at each end. As you get close to the line, you will see the waste wood start to crumble away on the surface (see above), showing that you are nearly at the line.

3 Cut a second piece of ash to approximately 605mm. This one will be cut to the exact length after the two pieces are glued together, so for now it can just be marked with pencil. The ends don't even have to be square at this point, as long as there is enough material to square them later. The face with the alignment marks will become the outside of the chest, so make it the nicer side. Try to make the grain patterns in each board flow into each other.

4 Check the edges sit together nicely. This is easiest with one piece held in the vice and the other resting on top.

Clean joins

It is good practice to use a plane to skim the edge of the boards where they join to remove any machine marks (see page 101). If the surfaces are not flat, the result can be an untidy glue line. If you are not confident doing this, and are happy the wood you are using has been nicely machined, you may be able to skip step 5.

5 Set the bench plane to take super-fine shavings and skim off one or two complete shavings along the length of the board. Watch the shaving as it emerges – you'll be able to see if you're taking off an even shaving. Bring up the other piece of ash to check how they sit. A very slight hollow along the length is acceptable, but we are talking a hairs' breadth. If the boards sit with gaps at the ends, you need to take some short shavings along the middle of the edges to make them sit together nicely.

6 Set up your sash clamps to the right size and cramp the board together to check the fit. If you are happy with the dry fit, remove the clamps, apply a neat layer of glue along the length of the shorter piece and then position it against the longer piece so it is hanging over an equal amount each end. Replace and tighten the clamps, and level the boards where they meet by feeling the join with your fingers and removing/ adding tension with the clamps to make the adjustment. Leave to dry, cleaning off the excess glue with a damp cloth or tissue.

Clamping tips

Pads underneath the clamp heads help protect the wood (see page 56), but you can simply avoid putting too much force on them instead.

Don't be tempted to just force the pieces together with the clamps as hard as you can to get rid of any gaps. This puts tension into the piece which will lead to a failure later on.

7 When dry, trim the upper part to length, with a 20mm overhang on each side. Use the shooting board and plane to trim the end down gradually – you could mark a line to aim for with the knife. (If there is a lot of wood to cut away, saw that off before using the shooting board). Use an offcut of the same wood to check the overhang is exactly right – since the board is the same thickness as the end panels will be, you know it's accurate.

8 Use the 25mm chisel gently to clean off any excess glue that has been squeezed out. Use the chisel bevel down and try to slice the glue away rather than just ploughing into it, as this can lift the grain. Avoid ramming the chisel along the grain – a shaving action is best.

9 Use a cabinet scraper to work over the join and complete the panel. Note how the scraper is held.

Sharpening a cabinet scraper

The general process for sharpening a scraper is to flatten and polish each face and long edge of the scraper on a sharpening stone to produce a smooth square edge, before consolidating the faces and edge with a burnisher. The burnisher (see pages 40–41) is then used to raise a burr on the edge; which is what gives the cutting action.

The burnisher is used to push the metal of the scraper around. Start by flattening the surfaces of the scraper on your 1,000 grit diamond stone. You only need to be working a section at most 20mm in from the edge. Hold the scraper edge-on against a square block of wood on the stone and move the scraper to and fro until the edge is square. If the edge isn't square, a burr can't be raised in the next step.

Lay the scraper on its face at the edge of your bench. Put a dab of lubricating oil (such as WD-40) on it to help it slide, then consolidate each face by applying heavy pressure with the burnisher, making twenty strokes on each side. Be sure to keep the burnisher in flat contact with the surface or you will round the edge. Next, wipe any oil off the scraper and secure it in your vice with the previously-squared edge uppermost. Run the burnisher square along this edge to consolidate it. You may feel a burr starting to form. Next apply the scraper to the edge again – but this time, to form the burr, draw the burnisher away from the edge, angling it down a few degrees off horizontal. Turn the scraper round in the vice and do the side of the edge. You should now have a burr on both edges that can be felt with your fingernail.

10 Make a second side panel in the same way.

11 For the first end panel, cut two lengths of ash to 420mm long, matching the grain patterns as before and adding a mark to show the faces and joining edges. If you are careful lining them up, you can just mark and cut both pieces to 420mm (using the saw and shooting board) before they are glued together. Watch for the pieces trying to slip past each other when you glue and clamp them – you might need to make an adjustment by loosening the clamps and then retightening when everything's in the right alignment. Make a second end panel in the same way.

12 Measure and mark the joint where the side panel will fit into the end panel. Choose which end of the end panel will be the top edge, then measure down 140mm from this edge and mark a line with the knife across the edge. Set the marking gauge to the thickness of the wood (20mm) and then draw it along the face, top and back of the panel, stopping where the 140mm line is. Extend the 140mm line with the knife onto the face and back of the panel. Mark the piece to be removed (i.e. the waste wood) in pencil, then repeat on the second panel.

Disguising the join

The grain should flow together: this means you are looking for similar sorts of patterns along the edges. If you use two pieces cut from the same board, this should be pretty easy.

Offcuts for precision

As in step 7, you can use an offcut of the same wood to ensure the 20mm measurement is exact.

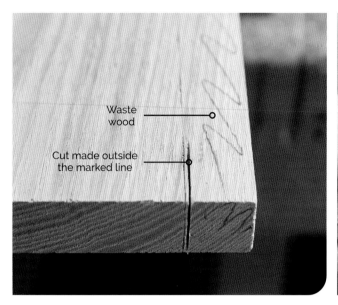

13 Start to cut out the waste wood by sawing 1mm or so away from the marking gauge line with the rip saw (make sure you're cutting in the waste wood). It is easiest to do this with the panel clamped down to the bench, rather than in the vice.

14 Use the 25mm chisel in a paring grip (see page 66) to clean down to the 20mm lines. It is easiest if you carefully press the chisel gently into the lines all the way round to create a perimeter. You can then slice away the waste wood that's left – don't go over the perimeter cuts and you will be fine.

15 Grip the chisel as shown and chisel back to the 140mm line. As before, cut a shallow perimeter section from each direction, then remove the wood in narrow slices to keep control before taking a couple of finer shavings across the whole surface to unify it as shown.

16 Very light use of the cabinet scraper can be helpful in getting rid of any minor bumps. Be wary of doing too much though, as you can lose accuracy.

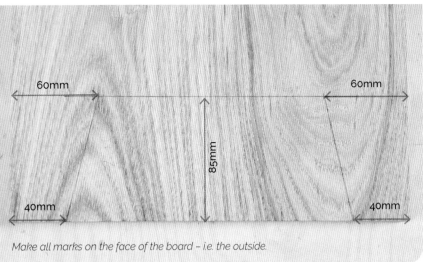

60mm   60mm

85mm

40mm   40mm

Make all marks on the face of the board – i.e. the outside.

17 Use a ruler and pencil to mark out the legs at the bottom of the panel, measuring 40mm in from each corner and a line 85mm up from the bottom. Measure 60mm in from each side along with line and mark, then draw lines from the bottom marks to the marks on the line, creating a trapezium (US trapezoid).

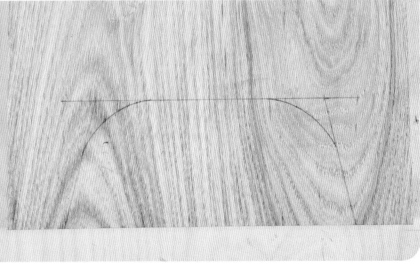

18 Use a tin of wax polish or similar round object to mark even curves, as shown. Allow for the offset of the pencil line away from the edge you are following – the pencil marks next to the tin, not right along the edge. Mark the leg cutout on the other panel in the same way.

GUIDES FOR THE COPING SAW

The coping saw is perfect for cutting small curves, as shown on page 56. However, its relatively coarse, long and shallow blade makes cutting straight lines with one difficult. Making the first part of the cuts with a small crosscut saw (see step 19) creates a guide for the coping saw to follow.

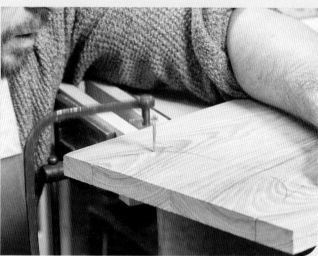

19 Use the small crosscut saw, guided by an offcut, to saw as much of the straight section of the leg cutout as you can. It's mainly the first few teeth on the saw that do the work – you can't go more than a few mm deep because of this – but making this cut will make it easier for the coping saw to follow neatly.

20 Use the rip saw to cut in along the other straight section, from the feet to just before the beginning of the curve. Next, slowly work the coping saw along the kerf. You might notice the kerf widening to the width of the different blade.

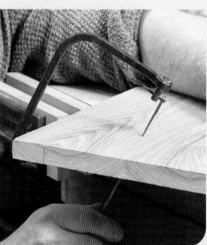

21 The coping saw is narrow enough to allow you to work around the curve. Be careful to keep the coping saw frame vertical as you go around the curve, and avoid applying lots of pressure as you cut: this will bend the saw blade and can make it cut a really unexpected line. Check on the underside from time to time, to check the blade is straight.

22 When you reach the straight part, adjust the angle of the saw to around 45° for greater control. Work along until the frame of the saw nears the wood as shown. You will find the straight but shallow cut you made in step 19 a great help: the blade will tend to follow it.

23 Rotate the blade relative to the frame in order to allow the frame to stand clear of the edge, as shown, as you work. Continue to the end of the straight, then follow the curve to the end, rotating the blade as necessary.

CLEANING CURVES

The coping saw leaves quite a rough surface so here are a few techniques for cleaning up the curves. Keep in mind that when the piece is finished, only the front edge and insides of the legs are visible, so pay particular attention to these areas.

Whichever tool you use for these cleaning cuts, be aware of the grain direction. The correct way is to cut from the flat mid-section down towards the feet. If you go the other way, you are cutting down into the grain and you risk chipping it. It is also much harder to get a clean cut.

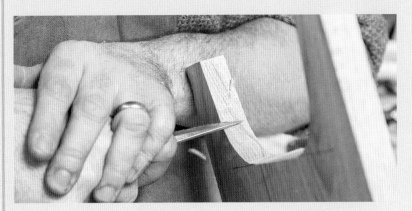

24 A Mora 106 knife is nice and narrow; ideal for sweeping around curves. With the end panel clamped securely, and with a two-handed grip on the knife, use a shearing action to work your way around the curve in long shavings with full control. Work from the flat bottom of the cutout towards the feet. Take the utmost care when using a carving knife like this. Always have in your head the thought, 'what happens if?' to try to stay aware of dangerous ways of working.

25 Change to a rasp and file for the flat section, working down to the mark made with the crosscut saw. A rasp is a nice and controllable way of cleaning up lumps and bumps in the curves too. Just beware of cutting straight across the edge as the back edge will be splintered. Use the rasp with a slightly sideways shearing action. Follow up with the file to remove the rasp cutting marks.

26 The cabinet scraper is useful yet again here, for a final light pass to smooth out the last bits. With a gentle touch, it works even on end grain.

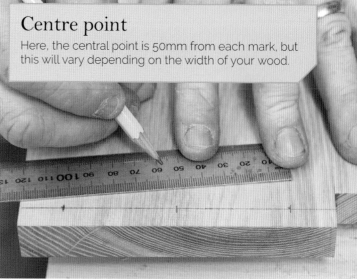

Centre point

Here, the central point is 50mm from each mark, but this will vary depending on the width of your wood.

27 Make a second end panel in the same way. Here are the two panels with everything cut.

28 Start marking out the positions of the dowels on the faces of the panels. Draw a line 10mm in from the end and then lay out the points along that line. 20mm in from each edge and then the middle between those two points. For the end panel marks, measure in another 140mm from the 140mm step. Lay out the marks in that space – they follow the same spacing as the marks on the side panels.

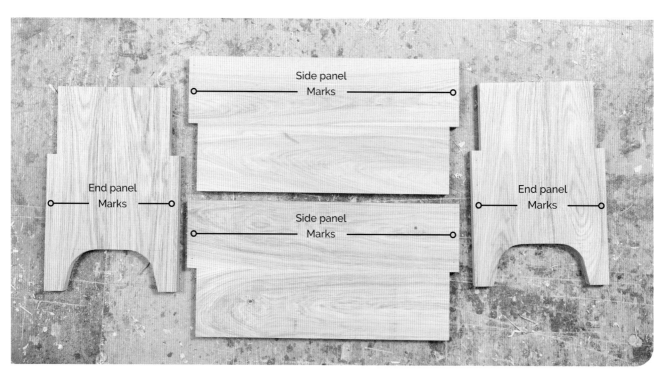

29 Mark up all the panels in this way.

30 Place the first panel on top of waste wood (drilling into this helps to ensure that the exit point doesn't splinter), then use a 4mm drill bit to drill the first point at an angle as shown.

31 Vary the angle for the marks at the other end. This will help hold the assembled box firmly.

32 Drill the central hole straight down.

Opposing angles

When I drilled these holes, I was looking along the panel from the end so that I could see if the position was square in that direction. Drilling the holes at opposing angles makes the joint much stronger.

33 Repeat the drilling on all of the pieces. Clean any splinters off the back of each panel.

34 Dry fit the box together and screw in 4 × 35mm screws into each of the central holes. Don't sink them in; just screw in enough to take up the slack.

35 Once you have checked the dry fit, unscrew the front and glue, then reassemble with lightly-tightened screws.

USING DOWELS

This chest is joined together using Miller dowels: precisely manufactured stepped dowels that are used in conjunction with a matching drill bit. They work like wooden nails, which have been around for a long time. You could use normal dowels but as they don't have a wider head section, they won't hold wood together as effectively. I am using mini dowels in walnut, to contrast with the lighter ash of the side and end panels.

The technique I have used takes advantage of the fact that the first section on the Miller bit is 4mm in diameter. By drilling 4mm holes through the pieces to be joined, gluing up and then pulling the chest together with a few screws as temporary clamps, I can then run the dowel bit in. Because it will be guided by the holes I have already carefully drilled on the bench, I don't need any big clamps to hold it.

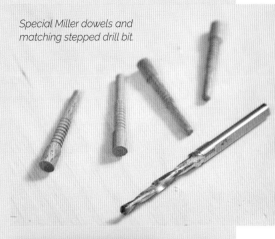

Special Miller dowels and matching stepped drill bit.

36 Change to the Miller dowel drill bit and drill out the top and bottom holes of one panel, leaving the screw in the central hole to hold things steady.

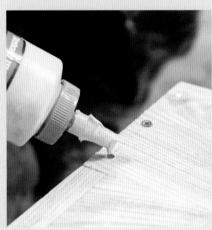

37 Drip a little glue into each hole.

38 Place a dowel in each hole and hit it with a hammer until the sound becomes dull – this indicates it is firmly wedged in place.

39 Remove the screw, drill out the central hole and knock in a mini dowel.

40 Wipe off any glue so as not to clog the saw teeth Use the flush-cut saw to trim each dowel flat.

The finished effect.

41 Repeat the dowelling process on the other panels in turn: gluing, drilling out the holes, then replacing the screws with dowels.

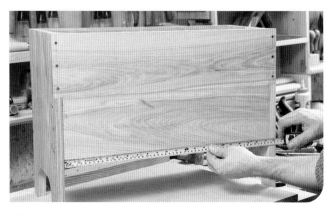

42 Measure the distance between the legs, then prepare another panel for the base, following the instructions earlier. Once glued, cleaned and cut to length, dry fit it. Check that the measurement is the same on both sides. If one side is longer, use that size. When dry fitting, the base should slide easily into place and not be putting lots of pressure on the corner joints.

43 Make a board for the lid, 12mm longer on each side than the box. Cut two pieces of ash to the width of the inside of the chest. These will be the cross batons that hold the lid in place. Mark the position that the batons need to go on the inside of the lid.

44 Trim the batons to fit. They should fit snugly within the box, staying in place when you remove your hand.

45 Line the chest up on the lid upside-down, with the battens in place. Draw a few small marks to show the edges of the chest where they line up, similar to when you made the small box project.

46 Mark each cross baton with lines 12mm in from each long side, then mark the line 25mm in from each end. Finally, mark the point equidistant between the 25mm marks. These are the positions for dowels to hold the piece in place.

47 Clamp the cross batons in place on the lid and follow steps 30–32 to drill the holes. Drive the middle holes in at angles too, to avoid working into the central joint in the lid panel. Be careful not to go too deep.

48 Drive the pegs into the lid using the hammer – remember to listen for the sound to become dull – then use the flush cut saw to trim away the excess. Note that the dowels are glued in, but the underside of the baton itself is not glued to the lid. This allows some expansion and contraction to take place.

49 Test fit the lid and plane down the edges if necessary.

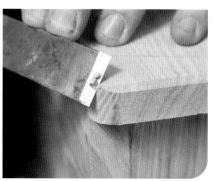

50 Use a small round object as a template then clip the corner off using the small crosscut saw. Finish the rounding with the rasp or chisel. Rasp along the grain; or shear across it with the chisel.

51 Round the corners off, then use the block plane to give chamfered edges to the top of the lid. You can mark a line to work up to, which will help to get this even. Round the edge over generously to make it more comfortable to sit on.

52 Use the chisel to chamfer the corner.

53 Chamfer the edges of the box, except for the lower eges of the sides – leave these as hard corners.

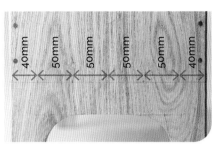

55 Mark up the sides with drilling points as shown above, then secure the sides of the base with dowels. The centre line of the holes is the middle of the base panel.

54 Glue the base in place, then secure it underneath with dowels in the same way as the sides (see steps 36–40), on a line 10mm in from the edge, and starting 50mm in from the box side. Space out the remaining dowels 110mm – you need plenty to ensure the base is securely held in place.

56 For a decorative finish, you can cut the ends of the lid at a 45° angle as shown, or shape it as you wish.

The finished chest.

INDEX